# The Accessible Museum

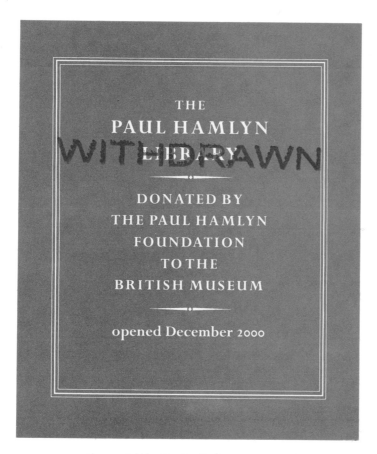

# *The Accessible Museum*

## Model programs of accessibility for disabled and older people

AMERICAN ASSOCIATION OF MUSEUMS

This book was produced with funding from the National Endowment for the Arts
and the Institute of Museum Services, federal agencies.

*The Accessible Museum*
Model Programs of Accessibility for Disabled and Older People

Printed in the United States of America
5 4 3 2 1   96 95 94 93 92

LIBRARY OF CONGRESS CATALOGING-IN-PUBLICATION DATA

The Accessible museum: model programs of accessibility
for disabled and older people.
p.      cm.
Includes bibliographical references and indexes.
ISBN 0-931201-16-0
1. Museums—United States—Access for the physically handicapped. 2. Museums and the handicapped—United States. I. American Association of Museums.
AM160.A27 1992
069'. 17'0973—DC20                92-29831 CIP

Compiling editor and interviewer: Marcia Sartwell. Coordinating editor: John Strand. Production editor: Amy Grissom. Associate coordinating editors: Donald Garfield, Susannah Cassedy. Bibliographer: Marina L. Rota. Indexer: Alice Fins. Designers: Meadows and Wiser, Washington, D.C. The Bauer Bodoni body typeface is 12 pt. throughout to accommodate readers with visual impairment. Printed by Expert/Brown, Richmond, Va.

PHOTO CREDITS: Cover: John Larson; p. 10: Museum of Fine Arts, Boston; pp. 19, 20, 23 and 25: John Mueller; p. 26: Children's Museum (Photo by David Powell, Spectrum Photography); p. 29: Children's Museum (Photo by John Cooper); p. 31: Bruce E. Millen; pp. 35, 37 and 39: Oraein Catledge; p. 40: Milledgeville-Baldwin Allied Arts; pp. 43, 46: Natural History Museum of Los Angeles County; pp. 48, 51: John Mueller; pp. 57–58: Aquarium of the Americas; p. 61: Donn Young; pp. 64, 66, 69 and 70: John Larson; p. 73: National Trust for Historic Preservation; p. 75: Oraien Catledge; p. 79: Jim Buck Ross Mississippi Agricultural and Forestry/National Agricultural Aviation Museum; pp. 81–82: Donn Young; p. 84: Oakland Museum (Photo by Joe Samberg); p. 87: Theodore R.M. Smith; p. 88: Oakland Museum (Photo by Joe Samberg); p. 91: Lowell Handler; p. 93: Winterthur Museum; pp. 94, 97 and 100: Lowell Handler; pp. 103–104: Kathleen MacQueen; p. 107: Lowell Handler; pp. 109, 112 and 115: Courtesy of Museum of Fine Arts, Boston; p. 116: Jim Collins; p. 119: Robert S. Arnold; pp. 124, 127: Theodore R.M. Smith; pp. 128, 130: M.H. de Young Memorial Museum; p. 132 and back cover: Jim Haisler; p. 135: Kimbell Art Museum (Photo by Michael Bodycomb); pp. 137–138: Jim Haisler; p. 140: Lawrence Hall of Science (Photo by Wallace Murray/Design Media); p. 146: Museum of Science, Boston; p. 153: Bruce Millen; pp. 154, 157: University Museum/Southern Illinois University.

*Cover: A visitor enjoys the beautiful Bloedel Reserve*
*Frontis: Guests chat on the deck at the Visitors Center*

# Contents

# Foreword

Museums across the country are working to make their collections more available to older adults and people who have various kinds of disabilities. Federal and state laws, including Section 504 of the 1973 Rehabilitation Act and the 1990 Americans with Disabilities Act, have accelerated the timetable for the transition in national attitudes and actions. The focus is inclusion: to open up existing programs and services and to reach out to underserved communities in ways that promote human dignity.

Museum professionals are now realizing that fully accessible facilities and exhibitions are making museums safer, more comfortable, and more meaningful for everyone. Ramps and elevators reduce accidents, accommodate baby carriages and carts, and are preferred by many who do not have disabilities. Large-print labeling with good contrast is meant to accommodate everyone. Captioned film and video heighten reading skills for children and foreign visitors; and exhibits presented at a height accessible to those who use wheelchairs are appreciated by adults of short stature and children as well.

This publication is designed to encourage and assist you in making your facilities and programs available to older Americans and individuals with disabilities whether they be staff, volunteers, creators, or audiences. The diverse museums profiled in this book are opening doors in ways that promote independence and dignity, and develop new and larger audiences. Each program confirms how close communication with disabled and older constituents increases accessibility in the most economical, efficient, and expedient manner. The selected bibliography provides resources to assist this process. Most important, this book demonstrates full inclusion of older adults and individuals with disabilities, not only in the featured profiles, but in the production of the book as panelists, writers, and photographers.

The creation of this unique book grew out of an agreement between the Institute of Museum Services (IMS) and the National Endowment for the Arts (NEA). In September 1986, the agencies agreed to work together "to advance the Federal agencies' common goal—to encourage and assists museums in making their collections and activities available to disabled people as mandated by Federal law."

Initially, the Endowment's Special Constituencies Office worked with the Smithsonian's National Museum of American Art (NMAA) to organize a nine-member advisory committee, composed of consumers with disabilities, accessibility experts, and staff to assist the NMAA in composing its National Survey of Accessibility in Museums that was funded by the Smithsonian Institution. This detailed survey was sent to 2,000 museums throughout the country, and 40 percent responded. This research, which was published in May 1989, uncovered a broad spectrum of exciting projects and resources. It not only provided the initial research for this book, but reinforced the need for such a publication. Subsequently, the Arts Endowment developed cooperative agreements with NMAA to compose the selected bibliography and the American Association of Museums to produce *The Accessible Museum*, which were jointly funded by NEA and IMS. AAM worked with the two agencies to convene a nine-member panel on November 29, 1990, which recommended the models documented in this publication out of a pool of 61 museums.

I hope *The Accessible Museum* will motivate readers to look more carefully at how they meet the needs of their older and disabled staff, volunteers, and visitors; to seek their advice in discovering where gaps exist; and to make any needed improvements so that every American may have the opportunity to experience this nation's cultural richness.

—*Daphne Wood Murray, Deputy Chairman for Public Partnership, NEA*

The American Association of Museums acknowledges with gratitude the following individuals who have contributed to the publication of *The Accessible Museum*: For the National Endowment for the Arts, Acting Chairman Anne-Imelda Radice and her predecessors John Frohnmayer and Frank Hodsoll, Kate L. Moore, and project director Paula Terry. For the Institute of Museum Services, Director Susannah Simpson Kent, former Director Lois Burke Shepard, and Rebecca Danvers; and for bibliographical research, Margaret Cogswell, and Mary Gregg Misch.

We extend our appreciation to the members of the Advisory Committee for the National Survey of Accessibility in Museums in the United States, conducted by the National Museum of American Art, Smithsonian Institution: Judith O'Sullivan, Margaret Cogswell, National Museum of American Art; Jan Majewski, Smithsonian Institution; Priscilla McCutcheon, Boulder, Colo.; Mary Ellen Munley, George Washington University; Mary Jane Owen, Disability Focus, Inc.; Margaret E. Porter, U.S. Dept. of Health and Human Services; Deborah M. Sonnenstrahl, Gallaudet University; Paula Terry, NEA; and Gail Weigl, Corcoran School of Art. For serving as chair of the selection panel, we thank Charles K. Steiner, Art Museum, Princeton University, and panelists Kathy Ball, Lafayette Natural History Museum and Planetarium; Ray Bloomer, Sagamore Hill National Historic Site; Karen Dummer, Children's Museum, St. Paul, Minn.; Lana Grant, Sac and Fox Library; Janet Kamien, Field Museum of Natural History; Dianne Pilgrim, Cooper-Hewitt, National Museum of Design; Beth Rudolph, Very Special Arts, New Mexico; and Deborah Sonnenstrahl.

At AAM we acknowledge the work of Kathy Dwyer Southern and Bill Anderson, and the research efforts of Nancy Hayward.

# Preface

DIANNE PILGRIM

*T*he publication of *The Accessible Museum* is an important achievement for the National Endowment for the Arts, the Institute of Museum Services, and the American Association of Museums. By directly addressing the specific issues of accessibility for museum audiences, the NEA and AAM endorse what we know to be at the core of all museums: they are for everyone. This simple declaration, an element of every public museum's mission, is one that is all too often overlooked. Barriers of all kinds—intellectual, social, cultural, and physical—prevent museums from fulfilling their potential as educational and cultural centers.

As a museum director with a physical disability, I observe these barriers and their impact from a unique perspective. I am concerned both with making the content and presentation of museum exhibitions accessible to the widest possible audience and ensuring physical access to the museum facility for each visitor. From the vantage point of my profession, my concern is that both of these issues be successfully addressed. But as I enter my own place of work in a wheelchair, via the back door, never having been able to mount the stairs leading to the museum's front door, I have a special interest in accessibility, particularly as it relates to the museum environment. This concern is not just about physical access, but it is about creating exhibitions and educational programs that are inclusive for people with visual and hearing impairments as well as learning disabilities.

I believe it is the combination of physical accommodation and mutual respect that is the important factor in making museums accessible. It is not enough to adhere to codes and requirements of door widths or TT (Telephone Texts for hearing impaired people). These architectural changes and improvements plus adaptive devices facilitate movement in a building and make the programs accessible to a wide audience, but more than the physical site must be changed. Our attitudes must be changed so that accommodation does not come only to equal inconvenience. Just because there's a ramp to the door, or a grab bar in the lavatory doesn't mean that the problems of accessibility have been solved. From museum guards to tour guides, curators to administrators, *all* of the public must be treated with dignity, courtesy, and human understanding. Our attitude must change to view the public as just that: a group of diverse people with various needs, concerns, abilities, and limitations.

My career in museums developed in a traditional manner—a love for the subject and eventually a desire to help chart the direction of an institution dedicated to design. I was diagnosed with multiple sclerosis in 1978 and have used a wheelchair for the past six years. During this time the word "accessibility" has taken on new meaning. It is not good enough for something to be just beautiful, it must function well also. Good design is about creative problem solving. We all need to be better designers when it comes to organizing museum exhibitions and educational programs.

This is a critical message. Our museums of art, design, science, and history should be accessible to everyone. The truth is that what is being done in the name of accessibility for persons with disabilities will make everyone's daily life easier. As our population ages, we will all come to appreciate the changes that the Americans with Disabilities Act requires.

Some of the most impressive programs in this book are the ones that are inclusive. Rather than devising projects for people with special needs (i.e. older people, visually impaired individuals, etc.), educational programs should speak to multiple voices, concerns, needs, and interests.

As we begin to see advocacy result in physical changes at our local supermarket, on the sidewalks, and in museums, we must also work to broach the other side of the question. We must make our attitude one of acceptance and respect. It is only with alteration and attitude that accessibility can be truly successful.

*Dianne Pilgrim is director of Cooper-Hewitt Museum,*
*The Smithsonian Institution's National Museum of Design, New York.*

# Introduction

CHARLES K. STEINER

*T*he *Accessible Museum* profiles nineteen American museums with relative availability to disabled people. It is intended to encourage museums to devise similarly creative ways to make their collections meaningful to a constituency that has not heretofore had the opportunity to take advantage of cultural offerings, especially those of museums. The goal of this particular essay is to lead the reader to approach the issues surrounding accessibility for disabled people in museums as a discipline or field of study, rather than as a prescribed and limited set of precepts required by law.

As a premise, the notion of accessibility for disabled people is still considered by some to be a radical idea: one can cite various news items on the alteration of mass transit (e.g., kneeling buses, elevators in subways) to substantiate the view that accessibility for disabled people is perceived as extreme or fanatic. This "radical idea" was legislated into federal law by the Vocational Rehabilitation Act of 1973, and its principles broadened and further articulated by the Americans with Disabilities Act of 1990. The often cited and critical portion of the Vocational Rehabilitation Act of 1973 says: "No otherwise qualified handicapped individual in the United States . . . shall, solely by reason of his handicap, be excluded from the participation in, be denied the benefits of, or be subjected to discrimination under any program or activity receiving federal financial assistance."

There are approximately 43 million disabled persons in the United States; it is estimated that one in five Americans have one or more impairments. The Arts Endowment's 504 Regulations define disabled persons as "any person who has a physical or mental impairment that substantially limits one or more life activities, has a record of such impairment, or is regarded as having such an impairment." In addi-

*Access to collections for disabled visitors fulfills the museum's democratic mandate.*

tion to widely introducing the concept of equal rights (including equal opportunity in employment) for disabled people, 504's other precepts include encouraging consultation with disabled persons (i.e., the consumers) in developing viable solutions to accessibility problems, and requiring institutions receiving federal support to prepare both a self-evaluation and a transition plan summarizing their current level of accessibility, and plans for improvement. While the legislation was not altogether successful, it did influence many museums, including those featured in this book, to consider disabled people as a viable potential audience and to explore various accommodations to make the constituency more comfortable in a museum setting. The Americans with Disabilities Act broadens the federal antidiscrimination mandate to all public services including public transportation, all public accommodations, including museums, and telecommunications. No longer may a museum opt to forego federal funding to avoid the steps or costs associated with making itself accessible to people with various disabilities.

The use of the term "disabled," while convenient as an abbreviation, is misleading because it implies a homogeneous subgroup of humanity. Everyone's disability is different and accessibility solutions that work for one person may not work for another. Further, there is sometimes an alienation between groups of disabled people such that a consensus on anything is impossible. The overlap between the population labeled as disabled and those labeled as senior citizens has always been sensitive; many older adults do not wish to identify themselves as disabled. Thus, there is frequently a schism between those over and those under 65 in self-perception; older adults who deny their physical limitations and the young who have, as the female lead in the Broadway hit *Children of a Lesser God*, a pride in their identity as "disabled."

Even within disability groups, there is frequently so much division that those who wish to deliver services to disabled individuals, like museums, have a very unclear focus. Among people who are deaf, there are those who communicate by sign language and those who won't; among blind people, there are those who support sheltered workshops and those who don't. There is a very great disassociation between disabled people who do and do not have neurological impairments, especially mental retardation. So frequently have the minds of people with physical limitations (blind, deaf, mobility impaired) been questioned, that they go to extraordinary lengths to disassociate themselves from people with mental disabilities. The British Broadcasting Company radio used to air a radio program called "Does He Take Sugar?" The title memorialized the waiter who asks a blind person's sighted escort how the blind person would like his tea, rather than the blind consumer himself.

Museum services for disabled people are not new, nor dependent on law. The Metropolitan Museum of Art, for example, has been serving such groups since 1913, when

Robert W. de Forest, Secretary of the Metropolitan Museum, offered two lectures on American sculpture and musical instruments, complete with touchable objects and braille. There are also records of the museum's "story hour for physically handicapped children" in 1924–25, and "lip reading lectures" in 1926. In the context of these Metropolitan Museum programs, what is really so new about the concept of museum accessibility for disabled people, and why has it taken all of us, disabled consumers and museum staff alike, so long to establish what has been popularly referred to as "cultural access"?

One answer is that the word "access" or "accessibility" has been overused and its meaning has become ambiguous in general usage. The term is also so closely associated with the Vocational Rehabilitation Act of 1973 that its underlying goal of integration has been lost by many. In turn, the need to comply with the law has sometimes eclipsed the philosophical and educational foundation for mixing disabled people into our society, including museums. (If asked to justify a particular program or architectural renovation, many museum professionals will answer "legal requirements" or "the law," without really knowing which law or any other legal specifications.) The mythic absoluteness associated with 504, which in fact proved to be so absolute that it required an additional piece of federal legislation—the ADA—precluded development of cultural access for disabled people as a discipline. Whereas art historians study the history of art or natural history curators study biology or botany and continue to do so throughout their careers in museums, few administrators expediting cultural access for disabled people in museums have reviewed anything but the most cursory surveys of solutions by other institutions. They may not have time to take the additional responsibility of 504 or ADA compliance, and, once more, they may not be particularly interested in the problem. Thus, the fiction of a prescribed solution is attractive. It also explains why, over the years, museums keep repeating the same mistakes and why the field of museum accessibility, or whatever we wish to call it, has moved forward ever so slowly—too slowly given the number of disabled people in the United States.

It is time to inject the field with new vocabulary, to evaluate methodology, to re-examine goals. Such a review should begin as it would in any other field, with a survey of the literature. Over the years, there have been influential books published by American and foreign museums or museum-related service organizations, authored by seminal figures in our discipline. To ensure improvement on past programs and progress in accessibility, these and other published volumes must be reviewed before proceeding.

One particularly important book is *The Principle of Normalization in Human Services* (1972) by Wolf Wolfensberger because it provides theoretical guidance in integrating disabled people into society from the point of view of institutions, mostly residential, that care for human beings. Instead of concentrating on aesthetic "concessions" that must be made to make services available to disabled people (e.g., lowering pedestals, enlarging typeface, etc.), the book concentrates on overall strategies for moving particular individuals from cloistered to less protective environments and lifestyles. In this author's view, it is unfortunate that so much of the literature aimed at accessibility in museums has stressed concessions, what museum staff often perceive as aesthetically negative changes. While the justification "everyone benefits" is always included in these rationalizations, the argument has not been convincing. Wolfensberger argues for integrating disabled people into society, but from a very different point of view, and in so doing, is of great help to those of us trying to devise strategies for incorporating disabled people into the museum-going public. So frequently, museums install a ramp or special program, but lack consistent overall accessibility to the museum.

Wolfensberger defines normalization as the "utilization of means which are as culturally normative as possible, in order to establish and/or maintain personal behaviors and characteristics which are as culturally normative as possible." He goes on to add:

"The normalization principle as stated is deceptively simple. Many individuals will agree to it whole-heartedly, while lacking awareness of even the most immediate and major corollaries and implications. Indeed, many human managers endorse the principle readily while engaging in practices quite opposed to it—without being aware of this discordance until the implications are spelled out. Then a manager may find himself in a very painful dilemma, endorsing simultaneously a principle, as well as practices opposed to it."

A prime example, in some museums, of the conflict between principle and practice is the appointment of a disabled person to teach other disabled individuals rather than nondisabled visitors in the public galleries. The principle of normalization would encourage the integration of disabled museum employees in jobs other than those which have exclusive contact with disabled visitors. Similarly, how would the normalization principle apply to special touch exhibitions of art in museums which do not normally allow touching? This is not to say that museums shouldn't hire disabled teachers or organize touch exhibitions; Wolfensberger emphasizes the importance of criteria and values in the decision to "normalize." The goals surrounding accessibility need to be clarified and museums must recognize their own biases as a profession in influencing the course of the discipline.

Is the issue before us accessibility, integration, and equality in a legal and a theoretical sense, or is it quality programming and contact with museum collections? A conflict arises here between these concepts from the museum's point of view. Most of us are concerned with bringing museum collections and disabled people closer together. At the same time, it is a fact that our museums have grown to become more than collections-centered institutions. Many museums have gift shops, parking lots, rest rooms, and restaurants, as well as sponsor parties and receptions. Many museum visitors, both able-bodied and disabled, come to museums expressly to take advantage of these services rather than to view the collections. Indeed, there is a fundamentally false assumption being made as a premise for many programs that are accessible to disabled people: that disabled people necessarily want to have contact with museum collections. As museum professionals, we only assume this premise because it is in the self-interest of museum professionals to do so; we do not allow disabled citizens the same rights of disinterest that we allow other visitors. Therefore, our discipline of accessibility has two subfields of study: facilitating integration in compliance with legislation (e.g., making buildings architecturally accessible and providing comparable services in an accessible location) and encouraging disabled people to use, enjoy, and learn from museum collections.

These, however, can be mutually exclusive ideas. To date, many museums have been using a museum program, often *one* museum program, such as a touch exhibition or the installation of a ramp, as a standard bearer or substitute solution to 504/ADA compliance. This has presented the government and the consumer with a quandary: on the one hand, it is heartening to see museums finally make a substantive gesture toward disabled audiences. But by condoning or complimenting the effort, are the consumer and government sanctioning the postponement of a necessary, broader, museum action toward accessibility? A corollary to this quandary is from the perspective of the museum professional. Suppose a curator believes the primary business of museums is collections-oriented and that the first aim of accessibility should be facilitating contact with the collections to the point of excluding the architectural alteration of gift shops or museum restaurants. Accessibility cannot be approached selectively but must parallel the functions, however diverse, of the museum.

This book, then, is a departure point, not an end in and of itself. The museum community should use it to further develop the field of disabled visitor services by understanding the need to become familiar with similar work being carried out by other museums, by treating the issues involved as they would other disciplines, and by exploring new solutions, while recognizing that the solutions established to date are imperfect, which is not to say not very good—but imperfect.

*Charles K. Steiner is associate director of the Art Museum, Princeton University*

# PART ONE

# Unique Outreach Programs

# Brookfield Zoo

*W*hen ten-year-old Mark entered the After-School Program at the Children's Zoo (a part of the Brookfield Zoo in Chicago), his therapist expected him to go on temper tantrums with kicking, screaming, and hitting, just as he had done in the past. Mark's behavior in the six-week program surprised everyone. He participated willingly in learning about and working with animals. Along with seven other children who had behavior disorders or learning disabilities, he milked goats, groomed horses, and held bottles of milk for young animals. And, he gave the staff no trouble.

Mark is just one of many individuals to benefit from the programs available for special populations at the Chicago Zoological Park, usually known as Brookfield Zoo.

In the early 1970s the Brookfield Zoo, like many institutions, became more aware of the needs of disabled persons, and it undertook the removal of barriers to these populations. During that decade it built ramps and inclines to provide access to buildings. It put up clear, easy-to-read signs, made paths level and wide enough for wheelchairs, and reserved parking areas for disabled visitors. For the benefit of visually impaired visitors, it issued large-print and Braille versions of some handouts and put Braille labels on many exhibits.

In the 1980s the zoo made rest rooms, telephones, drinking fountains, and restaurants accessible. It created a special-visitors brochure offering information on tours, wheelchair accessibility, handicapped parking, and other matters of interest to disabled zoo-goers. And it created the office of special populations coordinator and hired Mark Trieglaff, a former zoo-keeper who holds a degree in outdoor and therapeutic recreation, to fill it.

When Trieglaff took over the office in 1982, "special populations" meant persons

*Visitors board a trolley at the Brookfield Zoo.*

who were visually impaired, hearing-impaired, physically disabled, mentally retarded, and learning or behaviorally disordered. Now the audience has expanded to include the most severely disabled of those groups, plus individuals with autism, drug and alcohol abuse, and a variety of age-related disorders.

Trieglaff puts his goal in simple terms: "The whole intention," he says, "is to make the person's visit more enjoyable, a little easier, and to help them take advantage of opportunities at the zoo."

Many of the opportunities are closely tied with the Children's Zoo, which initiates most of the programs for special populations. With its collection of familiar domestic and native Midwestern animals, its hands-on approach, and its high keeper-to-visitor ratio, it is usually the first stop for visitors with special needs.

The staff assists visitors in approaching and touching most of the animals. "You can get a lot of hands-on contact with different animals, from the domestic ones like goats, horses, and chickens that you would find in a farm environment, to native animals like the armadillo," says Trieglaff. The armadillo is particularly popular because of its many different textures, such as its leathery outer covering, soft under-

*The zoo offers shuttle service for visitors.*

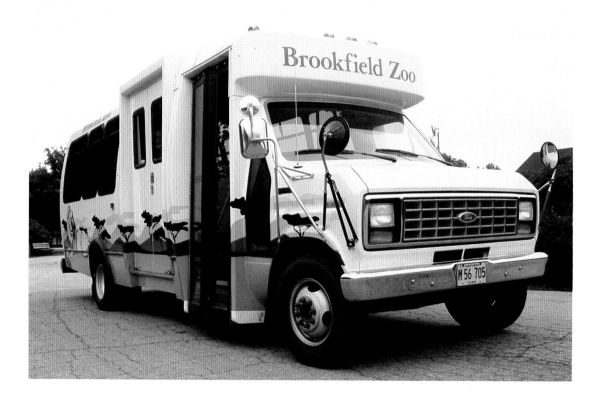

belly, and long, slender tongue, with which it sometimes licks the visitors' hands.

With such interaction, safety becomes a concern, but Trieglaff points out that zoo-keepers and volunteers instruct children and other visitors in the proper way to touch the animals, closely supervise all contact, and make sure the animals are never over-stressed. In addition, most of the animals have been raised by humans and are accustomed to being handled.

The Children's Zoo has also developed a number of sensory exhibits, used in conjunction with the tours, which special populations, as well as the rest of the public, enjoy. Taxidermied animals such as beavers, woodchucks, and opossums give visually impaired visitors a sense of animal shapes and textures. "Touch boxes" further heighten tactile awareness. Here visitors reach into covered boxes and run their hands across such items as a reindeer antler, cowhide, coral, starfish, coconut, or pine cone, then lift the lid to find out if they have identified the objects correctly. For visually impaired visitors, the answers are provided in Braille.

One section of "Sensory Corner" is devoted to the sense of sight. One display shows camouflaged animals; another shows the view of the world through a fish's eye and a bee's eye. In another section "smell boxes" challenge the visitor to identify odors ranging from pine to opossum to skunk.

The After-School Program is one of the Children's Zoo's most innovative and most successful initiatives. The program selects small groups of eight-to-twelve year olds, in cooperation with the West Suburban Special Recreation Association. Once a week the group learns about horses, dogs, and dairy animals, as well as the duties and responsibilities of those who care for animals. The children participate in such activities as trimming a dog's nails, cleaning a goat's stall, and brushing a dog's teeth.

The program culminates with each child presenting four different animals to the public in the Pet-and-Learn Circle. As part of their presentation, the children must answer questions the audience may ask about the animals. The aim of this exercise, and the program as a whole, is not only to educate the students, but to help them improve their social and listening skills and to boost their self-confidence, a commodity often in low supply.

"We've had a number of kids in the program who have had some serious behavioral problems and very low self-esteem," says Trieglaff. But after they work through the six-week course, he adds, "some of the kids start to look like professionals out there. They feel like, 'Hey, I know this information, and here's somebody who doesn't.'"

The close contact with animals helps students in a number of ways. Trieglaff reports that even children with severe behavioral problems in the classroom alter their behavior in the zoo program, probably as a result of heightened self-esteem. Follow-up evaluations show that this changed behavior often lasts beyond the conclusion of the program. Many participants who had not previously shown any interest in social or group activities have gone on to volunteer for the therapeutic riding classes or other animal programs, and some have even expressed an interest in working with animals in part-time jobs or as a career. Others have gotten pets.

While the program is designed to be primarily educational and recreational, its therapeutic benefits are undeniable. "That's not the intention of the program," says Trieglaff, "but it's an offshoot. It's definitely there." He finds support for his belief in recent research that documents how much disabled persons may benefit emotionally when they have animals around that they can observe and touch.

The philosophy behind animal-based therapy is that interaction with animals, particularly tactile interaction, can break through psychological barriers. The effects of a disability are rarely confined to one segment of a person's life. Hidden impairments, such as emotional or psychological disturbances, may stem from the reactions of others to the disability, thus creating barriers around the disabled individual.

According to the Brookfield Zoo's evaluation of its special-education programs, there are several reasons why contact between humans and animals can succeed in breaking through these barriers. First, the sensory experience, such as rubbing the rough trunk of an elephant, not only allows disabled people to reach beyond their everyday routine, but it also enhances their world by introducing them to powerful new sensations, a special benefit to those who may lack one or more senses. More important, for many disabled persons animals provide a complete acceptance and a disregard for their impairments.

Trieglaff tries to instill this sense of acceptance into zoo workers as well. He provides training to both full-time and seasonal employees, as well as to volunteers and docents who assist with tours and other programs for disabled visitors.

The training emphasizes empathy and knowledge. To help develop increased understanding for the challenges special populations face during their visits, workers and volunteers are sometimes blindfolded and taken on a tour or are left to navigate their way through the classroom in a wheelchair.

To heighten their knowledge of disabilities, they are given an in-house manual that includes guidelines for making presentations to different types of disabled groups. They learn, for example: "Blind is not deaf, so you need not shout. Also, blind is not dumb, so if you have a question for a blind person, ask him and not his companion." The manual also classifies and defines the major disabilities, provides general information about each, and discusses many misconceptions.

In the section on mental retardation, for example, staffers learn that of the eight million citizens of the United States that are considered mentally retarded, eighty-

*Ramps and inclines provide access to zoo buildings.*

nine percent are of high enough intelligence to function independently in society, and that one of the most effective ways to teach groups of retarded persons is to have them repeat information.

"Really, it's just a lot of common sense," says Trieglaff, "and getting the staff and volunteers to think in a common sense way about disabilities helps quite a bit in working with the groups."

Groups of disabled persons who wish to visit the zoo can call ahead and have a tour adapted to their particular needs. These tours focus on the Children's Zoo, with its many tactile exhibits, but may move on to the zoo's other facilities. They include Indian Lake, a man-made environment; the Seven Seas Panorama, highlighted by a wheelchair accessible area with a clear view of the dolphin show; and the Pachyderm House, where visitors get a close-up view of an elephant going through her exercises. This experience may be especially exciting to visually impaired persons, who from a distance might see only a grey blur but from a few feet away can see the elephant quite clearly and, with special arrangements with the zoo-keeper, may touch her.

The zoo makes these adapted tours available to a variety of disabled groups, but it has an ongoing relationship with a number of institutions serving special populations in the Chicago area. For example, the zoo provides a mobility-training practice ground for the Central Blind Rehabilitation Center at Hines Veteran Hospital. Groups of visually impaired veterans take tactile tours several times a year, and they are granted free admission to the zoo so they can practice moving independently in preparation for their release from the rehabilitation program.

In addition, Riveredge Hospital, the largest private psychiatric hospital in Illinois, provides patients from the alcohol and drug-abuse center to work at the zoo the second and fourth Friday of each month. While there, they receive information on the zoo's volunteer programs, and many continue to work as volunteers after they leave the hospital.

Other programs at Brookfield Zoo include vocational training and work-study opportunities for disabled individuals and "Senior Safari Tours" for older visitors. These tours are available to groups of twenty or more, and the nominal fee for this program includes general admission to the zoo, a dolphin show, and a reserved seat aboard a wheelchair-accessible tram.

For persons who cannot get to the zoo, the zoo has a program that it takes on the road. As part of its outreach program, the zoo staff visits such institutions as nursing homes and children's hospitals with an entourage of ferrets, armadillos, and skunks, as well as more common small animals such as dogs, cats, and rabbits. The presentations also include a sampling of tactile exhibits and handouts, usually in large print, which are left behind for the institution's library.

In a single year more than 6,000 persons with disabilities have been involved in programs at the zoo or have been visited as part of the outreach presentations. In addition, many other disabled persons have gone through the zoo on their own or with companions.

All programs for special populations at the zoo are followed up with evaluations from leaders of various groups, and the feedback has been overwhelmingly positive. A recent survey found that 100 percent of the group leaders said they would recommend the Brookfield Zoo to other special-population groups. Despite this high level of satisfaction, the staff is putting together an advisory group of agencies in the Chicago area to work on ways to improve the zoo for disabled persons. One of the aims of this panel will be to work together on securing grants and private funds to ensure the continued success of Brookfield's special-populations programming well into the future.

*A wheelchair accessible area offers a view of the dolphin show.*

# The Children's Museum

*W*hat If You Couldn't?—one of the most popular and enduring exhibits in The Children's Museum in Boston—helps youngsters understand what it is like to live with a disability by giving them a chance to experience it. In one part of the exhibit children are encouraged to climb into a wheelchair and try maneuvering it or pulling it up an incline.

In another exhibit the children may try to use a prosthetic arm which has been adapted to public use, or they may attempt to walk with the aid of metal crutches. Further on is a maze where blindfolded children learn firsthand about the frustrations of blindness as they feel their way along a multitextured wall. The experience of being "disabled" is nonthreatening and very brief, but the children gain some awareness of what life is like for persons who face these obstacles every day.

"What If You Couldn't?" was developed in 1979. "It was a landmark exhibit," says Nona Silver, special needs program coordinator. "It was clearly ahead of its time." A traveling version of the exhibit has appeared in a score of other museums and community centers throughout the United States and is still in use. An expanded version, which adds a videotape of fairy tales told in sign language, opened at the museum in January 1990.

Another exhibit that expands the visitor's understanding of disabilities is "My Mommy Drives a Wheelchair," the story, in black and white photographs, of Rosemary Larkin, who is quadriplegic. It begins with her decision to have a child and shows her raising her little girl Lorelei. "My guess is it reaches a lot of people," says Silver.

When it comes to reaching a large number of people and making them more sensitive to the needs of disabled persons, The Children's Museum does it as well as anybody and has been doing it longer than most.

~~~~~~~~~~~~~~~~~~~~~~~~~~~~~~~~~~~~~~~~~~~~~~~~~~~~~~~~~~~~~~~~~

*The Children's Museum occupies an 1888 waterfront warehouse.*

Founded in 1913 by the Science Teachers' Bureau, the museum was first installed in a city-owned building in Pine Bank, Jamaica Plain, a southwest Boston neighborhood. It is the second oldest such institution in the United States. With collections in natural history, the museum offered exhibits, lectures, loan kits, lantern slide presentations, and started a library.

By 1916 it was offering classes for children who were blind or deaf.

After outgrowing its second home in Jamaica Plains, in 1975 it joined with the Museum of Transportation to buy an abandoned warehouse on Boston's waterfront. Renovating the 1888 building, designing proper storage for the museum's 50,000-item collection (30,000 cultural artifacts and 20,000 natural history specimens), and building new exhibits took four years. During this period of design and reconstruction, says Silver, "accessibility for the disabled was uppermost in mind. For example, the exhibit Victorian House would not normally have a doorway a person in a wheelchair could get through, but when they built it, they made sure that it would work."

The museum does, in fact, have the type of easy accessibility that comes when it is built in, rather than added on later. Circulation routes through the museum have no curbs, steps, or protruding objects. Wheelchairs move easily through doorways. Elevators to the different levels are available, and call buttons can be reached from a wheelchair and read in Braille. Water fountains and telephones are accessible to those in wheelchairs, as are rest rooms (which have music from different cultures piped in). The old TT (Telephone-Text device for hearing-impaired persons) is being replaced by a new one that will operate twenty-four hours a day and will carry messages of upcoming events, so that a hearing-impaired caller will receive basically the same information that a hearing caller does.

Many museums, though, have similar features. What sets The Children's Museum apart is a truly welcoming quality that may have more to do with its philosophy than with its architecture.

The moment visitors enter, they sense they are welcome.

In most museums signs warn visitors not to touch. In The Children's Museum children are invited not just to touch, but to push, pull, operate, climb, explore, and experiment. Except for the Hall of Toys, where glass encases a collection of dolls, dollhouses, and toy soldiers, everything is "hands-on." Children clamor over the Giant's Desktop with its telephone the size of a rowboat, stilt-like pencils, and toddler-high paper clips. Children can pretend to be shopkeepers in a Latino market. They can examine the bones of various animals; climb on a two-story suspended sculpture; and make ocean-like waves and watch them break. They may be learning about

~~~~~~~~~~~~~~~~~~~~~~~~~~~~~~~~~~~~~~~~~~~~~~~~~~~~~~~~~~~~~~~~~~~~~~~

*Children learn about geometric shapes and cohesion at "Science Playground."*

THE CHILDREN'S MUSEUM

health, architecture, and science, but first of all they are having fun, and the decibel level in the museum proves it.

Something of the museum's philosophy is evident also in the number of exhibits on different cultures. Of these the most remarkable may be the *Kyono machiya*, the 150-year-old home of a Japanese silk merchant. It was dismantled in Kyoto, Japan and reassembled in the museum by Kyoto craftsmen. With its adjoining street and garden, it offers a rare opportunity to learn about Japanese life and architecture and to compare modern lifestyles with traditional ones.

The exhibition on American Indians helps children look past the stereotype of Indians in feathers and war paint. On one side of the room is a wigwam large enough to hold eight to ten children; on the other side is a small contemporary clapboard home with life-size paintings of Indians wearing jeans and T-shirts. While seeing how Indians live in today's world, children also learn something of their traditional values—respect for the earth and for all living creatures.

The Victorian house, which used to be called "Grandparents' House," is now called "The Gutermans' House". The furnishings, food, and knickknacks show how a Jewish family might have lived in the pre-World War II era. Children can explore through the house that stretches from the museum's second to the fourth floor. The house has a cellar, a living room, and an attic full of treasures from another era.

"Kids' Bridge," a new exhibit, provides a powerful experience about prejudice, racism, and culture. The bridge, a forty-six inch span, leads visitors into a dramatic environment suggesting greater Boston. With two screens and a computerized tracking ball, visitors take part in a "treasure hunt" through five ethnic neighborhoods with children from those neighborhoods as guides. Whether searching in Revere for Cambodian food or in Roxbury for an African medallion or playing cross-cultural games, they gain a new understanding of different cultural ways.

"For children who will be adults in the twenty-first century, learning to see themselves and others as part of a culturally and racially diverse society may be as important as learning to read," says Kenneth Brecher, director of The Children's Museum.

"We have always tried to reach a broad audience," says Nona Silver, "and reaching people who are disabled is just part of that process."

Wednesday mornings during the school year are reserved for visits from groups with special needs. One group is scheduled at 9:30 and another at 10:45. To make sure that the children receive the maximum benefit from their visit, the groups are kept small—no more than thirty—and several museum interpreters accompany them.

The museum interpreters, who are key to the success of the Wednesday morning program, receive intensive training in special needs issues ranging from interacting with hearing-impaired children to understanding dyslexia. The interpreters are salaried employees. Many have previous experience in helping disabled persons. Some know sign language. All interpreters participate in regular weekly training sessions. These include guidance about specific areas of special needs as well as group discussions. Here interpreters may discuss their feelings and work on different ways to handle problems that have arisen.

Interpreters adapt the tour according to their assessment of what will be most enjoyable and beneficial to the children in their charge. Interpreters need to be able to make this judgment within a few minutes after the children arrive.

Disabled children can participate in many ways in the museum. A visually impaired child, for example, might enjoy exploring the Giant's Desktop, discovering the big buttons on the big telephone. From there, she could go to the "Bones" exhibit, where she could handle bones from different animals. At the Raceways Exhibit, which is about motion and momentum, golf balls move at different speeds on various types of tracks, such as a spiral and a roller coaster. The visually impaired youngster can feel both the ball and the tracks and can hear where the ball is from

*A young visitor tries out a touch screen.*

start to finish. And for both hearing and hearing-impaired children, there is an area for watching videotapes of fairy tales told in sign language.

Sometimes children who are not expected to get much out of their experience surprise everyone. "I was talking to a teacher near the 'Bones' exhibit," says Nona Silver. "There's a light table, and we put x-rays up. One of the boys in her class began naming the bones, and it became clear that he had learned every bone in the body. The teacher was stunned. 'I can hardly believe this,' she said. 'This boy is all over the classroom. He never sits down.'

"We get a lot of the kids who are behavior problems in the classroom, and it's not evident here. They get caught up in the exhibits. I've heard the teachers say, 'You're going to have to keep your eye on him every minute,' and then nothing happens."

In addition to the exhibits, the museum holds Friday night musicals or storytelling performances by guest artists. "Magic: Possible Impossibilities," with Erik Wikstrom; "Meet the Composer," with David Polansky; and "Magical Melodies with Puppets," with Wendy Frank are typical offerings. At least one performance each month is signed for the benefit of hearing-impaired children. The museum also sponsors the Boston engagement of the Big Apple Circus, which offers several signed performances.

Working with the Very Special Arts (VSA) organization, the museum hosts a one-day children's festival in the arts. About twenty local artists are stationed in the exhibition areas of the museum. More than 600 children from special education and regular classrooms, go to four different sessions—face-painting, puppet-making, clay, and performing arts—where they create their own art under the supervision of these artists.

In one year the museum's Wednesday morning program serves about 2,000 children and adults. Other disabled persons go through the museum with their families or as part of summer camp programs. The influence of the museum's program, however, extends far beyond the number of children who are directly served by it.

It is not possible to separate out all the costs of the special services and programs from the $5.9 million budget of The Children's Museum. The costs of an exhibit on disability awareness, for example, are calculated with the other exhibits. Staff costs for the program, however, appear modest, particularly for so influential a program. Forty percent of Coordinator Nona Silver's time is devoted to accessible programming, plus the Wednesday mornings of ten to fifteen interpreters.

The museum is a valuable resource to the community, especially its schools, and to other museums. Since 1964 it has made its materials available, for a modest rental fee, in the form of kits, which Silver describes as "miniprograms that extend their visits into the classroom." Kits include lesson plans, activities, objects, artifacts, models, and audio-visual materials. Educators may choose from ninety topics. Six of these are concerned with disability awareness. The kits are rented through the Resource Center, which also has an extensive collection of books, periodicals, and audio-visual materials available to the public.

The museum holds workshops and seminars for teachers on topics in science, culture, and child development. Seminars on disability awareness are frequently offered. In the spring of 1990 one seminar focused on issues that arise as mainstreaming of children with special needs continues in the public schools. Earlier, with a three-year grant from the Foundation for Children with Learning Disabilities, the museum instituted a training program for public school teachers to increase their skills and level of comfort when working with children with learning disabilities.

With Old Sturbridge Village (see separate chapter on this site) The Children's Museum co-founded the Access Network for Museums. This is a national network of museum professionals who meet periodically to discuss physical, programmatic, and attitudinal barriers to accessibility within museums.

About 500,000 visitors come to the museum each year, and another 250,000 teachers, community workers, parents, and children in communities throughout New England are reached by its outreach services.

To Nona Silver, however, the impact of The Children's Museum is best summarized in the story of the Latino boy whose class was visiting "The Clubhouse," an exhibition area for children ages nine to fifteen. He was on the dance floor of "Recollections," an exhibit where music is piped in and a laser beam throws colored images of a person's movement on a reflective screen. Suddenly, inspired by the music, the movement, and the images, he began talking to his classmates. His teacher stopped her own conversation in mid-sentence. "Wait, wait, wait . . . " she said, "I never heard that child speak before."

"For this boy, it was a real breakthrough," says Silver. "It's times like that that fill you with awe."

# The John Marlor Arts Center/Allied Arts

*T*f there were such a thing as a spirit of accessibility, it would undoubtedly reside in Milledgeville, Georgia, population 13,500. Milledgeville, the former capital of Georgia, is a town with a proud past. In its Historic District the visitor can see the former State Capitol, which served as the seat of government from 1803 to 1868, the Old Governor's Mansion, and scores of antebellum structures with their trellised balconies, colossal porticos, Doric columns, and ancient cedar trees. Milledgeville even gave its name to a unique architectural genre—Milledgeville Federal, a blend of late Georgian, Federal, and early Greek Revival styles.

Today Milledgeville is the setting for lively and diverse programming in the arts—programming that not only reaches the entire community but is free of charge about ninety percent of the time.

The organization that makes all this happen is called Milledgeville-Baldwin County Allied Arts, a nonprofit agency charged with the dual purposes of making a variety of experiences in the arts available to local citizens as well as managing the John Marlor Arts Center properties, a cluster of historic buildings that date from the years 1810–1830. Allied Arts' commitment to accessibility is not only very direct and no-nonsense; there is something personal and small-town homey about it as well. No government organization has been breathing down the back of Allied Arts about accessibility. The agency seems to have made things accessible because that's the way they want it, and they want it that way because they know some nice folks who happen to be disabled whom they do not want to inconvenience or leave out of anything.

Allied Arts acquired these buildings in the late 1970s through matching grants

*Making the historic John Marlor House accessible proved challenging.*

34

secured from the Department of Natural Resources and the Department of Housing and Urban Development for the development of threatened historic properties. A fourth historic building was given to the arts program by private citizens, Mr. and Mrs. Floyd Griffin. Deeds for all four properties were signed over to the City of Milledgeville for the use of the arts agency.

The most significant of these properties is the John Marlor House at 201 North Wayne Street, home of the English master builder John Marlor and a fine example of Milledgeville Federal. Since 1979 it has housed the Allied Arts offices and the Elizabeth Marlor Bethune Art Gallery.

Returning this building to its original form and making it accessible were among Allied Arts' first priorities. "When we first got this property, there were all kind of apartments tacked up on the shed roof and over the breezeway," says Betty Snyder, director of Allied Arts.

Among the changes carried out to make the building accessible were the alteration of the front steps from five to six in order to make the rise safer and more comfortable; dismantling the breezeway connecting the main house with the kitchen section, then lifting the old kitchen eight and one-half inches onto new piers and re-attaching it with a new breezeway to the original 1830 section; installing two accessible bathrooms; adding a ramp and bannister rail; and adding a concrete walkway to make direct connections from the house to the new accessible parking area.

Asked if this meant that wheelchair users had to enter through the back door, Betty Snyder replied, "Yes, that's right, but all our friends come in the back door. That's where the off-street parking is; nobody comes in the front door except people who don't know us very well."

Working with Special Audiences, Inc., Allied Arts next did a photographic survey to determine the accessibility of all the places in town where it might wish to sponsor performances, exhibits, classes, or workshops. Some of them were not accessible. Allied Arts has a very simple, effective policy about this. "They are now," says Snyder. "Otherwise, we don't use them."

Take the accessible restrooms in the John Marlor Arts Center, for example. It was important to get them in quickly because David Sampson, a visual artist, was opening an exhibit there. "David is in a wheelchair," says Snyder, "and he has trouble moving his arms, so he works slowly. Once he gave a demonstration of how he works, and it goes almost at a snail's pace. Then when you look at his finished works and realize what he turns out—it made a tremendous impression on us. So, of course, when he did an exhibit here, we wanted to have a restroom that a wheelchair could turn around in."

Then there was the ramp. "We didn't know it was slick under certain conditions until we had a person in a wheelchair use it and it was slippery for her. So now every one of those boards has this little grit strip you put across it. Experience has made us more aware of some of these things."

There was also the lady who was deaf and visually impaired. "So we thought, 'How can we help her be more self-sufficient when she comes in?'" says Snyder. "We wanted her to know her way around without someone always staying with her; you know, that bothers a person, like at a store when someone follows you around. We had a drawing from the architect showing the layout of the gallery spaces in the main building. We put it in one of those plastic frames, and then took a glue gun and drew the lines on it so that you can feel the raised lines showing

*Visitors entering the John Marlor House.*

the layout. We did it for that one person, but now we have it for anybody else."

For all this, though, the second floor of the John Marlor Arts Center is not accessible to wheelchairs because the circular stairway is too steep for a ramp, and putting in an elevator would mar the historic integrity of the structure. The second floor, however, is used primarily for offices.

Considering the size of the community, the arts programming in the Milledgeville-Baldwin County area is surprising not only for its diversity but for the fact that it touches virtually every part of the community. There is a certain amount of standard programming: Each season features about ten performances of such groups as the Southern Ballet Theatre and The Gregg Smith Singers in the "Town and Gown" concert series. The "gown" part is the coed Georgia College. About twenty-five art exhibitions are held either in the Marlor Arts Center or in satellite sites (usually the Mary Vinson Memorial Library) or on tour. One of the exhibits, "Black Women: Achievements Against the Odds," was co-sponsored by the museum, Archives of Georgia Education, and the Smithsonian Anacostia Neighborhood Museum.

The extent of the outreach into the schools is noteworthy. In the 1989–1990 season, for example, Allied Arts presented sixteen in-school performances, including the Pandean Players, Poetry Alive! and Tell Tale Theatre. In addition, eight artists served residences in the schools and community for periods ranging from one to six weeks. These artists included pottery artist George Lea, theater artist John Schmedes, photographer Larry Erb, sculptor Gregor Turk, and visual artist Tom Ferguson.

School-age children are also reached through at least four different summer camp programs. Each program lasts five days, and at least four are offered during the summer. A typical offering is the Science and Writing Camp, in which field biologist and author Jack Nisbet helps children explore the nature of the region and then guides them in writing about what they have seen.

Since artists in residence teach classes in the community as well as in the schools, Milledgeville adults always have a broad selection of interesting offerings from which to choose. In the 1989–1990 season classes or workshops were offered in watercolor painting, choral singing, basket making, tap dancing, portrait painting, crafts, bird carving, and writing.

A number of older adults take part in these classes; for those who cannot come to the center, outreach classes are given at the Senior Citizens Center or at the retirement home. Classes are also given at Unity Place, a sheltered living environment for disabled and/or disadvantaged persons.

Allied Arts is also one of the sponsors of the Very Special Arts Festival, where

*The tombstone of master builder John Marlor.*

artists help children with physical or mental disabilities get involved in arts and crafts. At a recent festival, Allied Arts hired Rusty Redfern of Atlanta to give a demonstration of drawing. Since Rusty, who has no arms, draws with his feet, the demonstration was enlightening for the children.

Allied Arts takes pride in its ability to come up with new ideas. Three recent programs illustrate novel ways to use arts programming to benefit special groups—in these cases, teachers, inmates, and latch-key kids.

Teachers would seem to need no special help to enjoy the arts, but the premise of the artist-teacher training program is valid. Since there will never be enough

*The John Marlor House.*

artists-in-residence to reach all children, the idea is to teach teachers how to integrate the arts into their classrooms. Starting in 1990, some of the artists in residence teach summer classes for teachers on such topics as how to use video, drama in the classroom, Southern literature, and reading and writing for teachers. The classes run for seven intense days. Even though the classes provide no teacher credit, the number of teachers taking the courses doubled in 1991.

In 1989 Allied Arts sent artist in residence John Schmedes to teach a class in theatrical improvisation at Rivers Correctional Institute. These classes went so well that the corrections recreation services contracted with Allied Arts for Schmedes to create a pilot program in theatrical techniques. The workshops, held twice weekly for six weeks, included fifteen inmates. According to Bill Hinton, assistant director of recreation services, the prisoners' "communication skills and self-confidence improved with every session." He added, "We also saw a gradual movement away from 'criminal scenarios' in their improvisations." Both Allied Arts and Corrections plan to continue co-sponsoring the program while also expanding into other arts disciplines.

At the women's prison, creative writing took hold, thanks to workshops from poet Al Masterick (editor of the journal *Swamproot*) and novelist Judith Ortiz Cofer *(The Line of the Sun)*. So much of the work that the women in prison created was good that Allied Arts considered putting out a book of prison writings but scrapped that idea in favor of a better plan. "We have a writers' group in town working with these different writers as they come through," explains Snyder. "So what we are going to do is put out a book of regional writing by people in Baldwin County, and we're not going to say which writers are in prison or which ones are in town. We'll use names but no addresses. It doesn't matter where the writers are — only that they write well."

The Art after School program, launched in September 1991 with African dancer and storyteller Deborah Ferguson, also uses artists-in-residence in an innovative way. As the title implies, the art classes will take place after school, and the program is intended to benefit latch-key kids who often have no place to go then.

The liveliness of the arts in Milledgeville is due not just to Allied Arts, but also to the many groups that co-sponsor events. These groups include the City of Milledgeville, the Baldwin County School System, the Georgia Council for the Arts, the Artists-in-Education Program, the Mary Vinson Memorial Library, the Georgia Humanities Council, the Southern Arts Federation, and Georgia College. The organization also has an active group of volunteers, Friends of Allied Arts, and a strong base of support from the City of Milledgeville, which contributes forty-seven percent of its approximately $200,000 budget. To Allied Arts, however, goes credit for using its resources to produce arts programming that touches every level of life in the Milledgeville-Baldwin County area.

# Natural History Museum of Los Angeles County

*W*hen the half dozen docents pack up their storyboards, videos, and museum artifacts and pile back into the Natural History Museum's van, they always leave behind a group of people who are more interested, more animated, and more outgoing than they were before. And this is true whether the docents are returning from a special education classroom for disabled children or a nursing home for older people.

"The teachers tell us that after the presentation the children talk more with each other," says Jennifer Bevington, who coordinated the outreach programs for disabled children and seniors for three years. "That's something that happens also with the Senior Outreach Program. Many times people in these facilities do not have family to visit, and they feel very alone, forgetting that one resource is the person sitting next to them. One of the things we've seen over and over is that after our presentation people begin talking with each other."

The two groups have something else in common. No members of either group are ever likely to come to the museum on their own. The children have physical, mental, emotional, or developmental disabilities; the older people often have medical problems and difficulty in traveling. If these groups are to have any experience of a museum, the museum must go to them.

And the museum does provide outreach with programs that are so appealing it is easy to see why the participants respond. For disabled children, there are three presentations: Dinosaurs, Life in the Ocean, and North American Mammals. Working with a group of about nine children, docents first capture their attention by using brightly colored illustrations on a large velcro storyboard to present the basic concepts. Then, the children get to touch—as well as smell, han-

*Dinosaur presentations are available for disabled children.*

dle, and play with—the artifacts and specimens from the museum's collection.

In the dinosaur presentation, for example, the children handle a full-scale model of an allosaurus skull with three-inch teeth, real dinosaur bones, and a huge sea turtle shell, which they sometimes put on their backs as they walk around while they pretend to be turtles.

The objects are both valuable and breakable, but the museum intentionally takes the risk, so important is the children's involvement. "From time-to-time some of these bones have to be replaced," says Bevington, "because they get a lot of loving."

"Life in the Ocean" is a "sensory experience," says Bevington, one that opens up new worlds for some of the children. "Everything smells like the sea. We've got a bottle of krill, and it fascinates the kids to learn that the largest mammal on earth eats one of the smallest ones. We've got vertebrates and invertebrates, and things like shark skins and shark egg cases.

"Often docents who live by the beach will get some kelp that's fresh and has the ocean smell. Or, they will bring sand—it's amazing the number of kids who live in Los Angeles who have never been to the ocean. And there are different fish models, anemones and sea shells. We also talk about things that live near the ocean—the sea birds, the marine mammals, and the life in the tide pools. It's a cut through the ecosystem."

Three times each month a group of four to six docents presents these programs at different schools in the county that include children with various disabilities. The presentation lasts about one hour, so the docents may reach several classrooms in one morning's work. They work together in the classroom because the classes need a high ratio of adults to students, and, as Bevington puts it, "it takes a lot of hands to do the program."

Afterwards, the docents usually go out for coffee to talk about any difficult problems or any child in need of special attention. "They need to debrief," says Bevington. "There is a real camaraderie among the people who do the program. Not everybody can do it. It's tough to walk into the classrooms and see these kids."

An unusual aspect of the program is that it was developed by volunteers, working with museum staff. "The program was modeled after one at The Carnegie in Pittsburgh," says Bevington. "One of our docents was from The Carnegie, and she wanted to duplicate it at Los Angeles, although it has been adapted to the different circumstances. There is a core group of about fifty docents who are very involved and very committed to it."

Equally unusual is the way the docents are trained for the outreach programs. They must first go through the full year of training required of all docents. Then, they generally guide tours for a year. After that, they are encouraged to do the outreach programs. If they choose to do so, they are trained by the more experienced docents. "They learn through observation and spending time with the older docents in the classroom," say Bevington. "It's one of the most successful things we have done. It's really effective if you are taught by someone who's good."

The funding came in part from National Medical Enterprises, which gave the museum a grant of $22,000 in 1985 to start the program and keep it running for three years. The money paid for the van ($14,000), the artwork and display boards ($4,500), printing brochures ($2,000), and some "touchable" items. A similar grant in 1990 underwrote part of the salary of the outreach coordinator and paid for some of the program's expenses. The rest of the program's $15,000 annual operating budget comes from museum funds.

The program for seniors is even more of a bargain. Most of the start-up costs were donated—the van was a gift from Beverly Enterprises, and individuals supplied many of the artifacts. The museum paid $3,000 for the background sets and costumes and picks up the $10,000 annual operating costs.

For all their similarities, however, the program for seniors is more unusual—and more difficult—than the program for children because here the museum has deliberately aimed at a segment of the population most likely to be ignored—older people who reside in institutions.

It was a carefully thought-out decision. "When you start working with outreach programs, you have to question who you are and what you are doing," says Bevington. "We are an inner-city museum, and our mandate is to serve as much of the public as we can. You have to ask: 'What is the goal? To reach people who never heard of the museum or who might be intimidated by it? Or to reach people who can't come here at all?' We chose to go to the immobile elderly who will never come to the museum because they can't."

In developing a program for this audience, Bevington worked with a staff member, Isabel Rosenbaum, who was completing an advanced degree in gerontology at the time. Clearly, a lot of understanding of older people undergirds the program and is evident not just in what is presented but in how it is presented.

What type of program will interest people who are quite old and probably not very well? The real problem, says Bevington, is not that they are old: "Learning doesn't stop," she says. "Research shows that your ability to learn may drop slightly, but you are still able to acquire new information." The problem is that "more often than not the residents are over-medicated or under-stimulated, or both," and sometimes they have "just shut down."

Two presentations work very well to kindle their interest and participation. One is "A Walk in the Wild," an armchair nature walk through the chaparral, a native

*Special programs allow children hands-on experience.*

southern California plant and animal community. Using taxidermied specimens from the museum's collection, the docents pass around examples of the wildlife that inhabits the area—skunk, fox, gopher, rabbit, scorpion and birds—and encourage the residents to touch them and talk about what they have. The presentation ends with a videotape that enables residents to see the wildlife and hear the sounds of the chaparral.

Docents are encouraged as they present the program to touch the residents, says Bevington, "to put their hands on the person's shoulder, to pick up his hand and place it on some of the objects being passed around. Just to be touched and talked to is helpful for some of these people."

The second program, "Do You Remember When?" focuses on the year 1913. Two backdrops are used—one of a kitchen and one of a garage. Docents begin by talking about some of the things that were going on that year—the war, the digging of the Panama Canal, the inventions, the beginnings of a movie industry. Then they narrow the subject down to the home and family life. "What were your mother and grandmother doing in the kitchen?" they ask, passing around kitchen objects from the period. Sometimes the objects look like the ones we use today (eggbeaters have not changed much, for example), but others come from a different era—the washboards, the sock stretchers, the big wooden stirrers used while doing laundry in a vat of boiling water.

"The best part is the costumes," says Bevington. "One is a housedress that you would wear while working at home. We also have an opera coat, with a headband and ostrich feather, as well as a bathing costume—it's this huge thing with bloomers and a skirt and a big hat. Some of the docents wear those, and it's always great for yuks. People wake up and laugh.

"They talk about the music that was popular then, and sometimes people will start singing if they remember a song. Sometimes the docents ask where people were in 1913, and there is always someone who came from another country and tells his story about coming to the United States and settling in Los Angeles. So we get people sharing their stories."

Bevington is forthright about the depressing aspects of some of the institutions they visit: "We've gone into a range of homes, and we've seen everything from places where the smell of urine is just overwhelming and everybody is tied in his wheelchair, wearing diapers, and overmedicated, to places that are just wonderful. There is one home in West Hollywood that has a fantastic activity director, and every year she brings in the Chippendales—the male strippers. I tell you, it's dynamite. That's not the only thing she does, of course, but she brings that kind of energy to the job."

It has not been easy to get docents to present this program, and Bevington is insightful as to the reasons: "If you look at the average docent, you find someone who is getting on in life. And what they find when they go into these homes is that they are facing themselves. It's really difficult. The program for seniors hits close to home.

"I think for the residents one of the biggest impacts of the program is that somebody is talking to them and paying attention. They give you this look that is almost beyond words, that says, 'You have shown an interest in me. I'm a human being.'"

# Spertus Museum of Judaica

Around a table in the Spertus Museum of Judaica are half a dozen older men and women carefully examining objects that illustrate aspects of Jewish life—Torah scrolls wrapped in velvet and decorated with silver, candle holders and oil lamps used on the Sabbath and Hannukah, a prayer shawl, or *tallith*. These are participants in one of the museum's Leisure Tours, designed especially for older adults and for visually impaired visitors. In fact, though, these Leisure Tours involve no touring. Senior adults who are not up to walking from showcase to showcase ensconce themselves in comfortable chairs while a docent brings selected objects from the collection to them.

The museum's permanent collection specializes in objects that illustrate life in the synagogue, objects that are used in the home to celebrate the Sabbath and the Jewish holidays, and objects that celebrate such life-cycle events as birth, coming of age, marriage, death, and mourning. Most of the objects date from the nineteenth or twentieth century, but the museum also has a special archaeological collection of ancient artifacts, which are taken out for special occasions.

The experience of holding some of these objects is especially meaningful to some of the older Jewish men and women. "There was a time when women were not permitted to participate in the rituals in which these objects were used," says Education Curator Kathi Lieb. "That has changed in America in many communities. So, when we pass around a Torah scroll to a seventy or eighty-year-old woman, this may be the first time she has ever touched it. It can be a very moving experience for her. It can be a significant experience for men, too, who perhaps have not participated in a synagogue since they've been in a nursing home, or have participated only on major holidays.

*A silver ark used for holding the Torah.*

"We also have the familiar things used in the home—metal boxes used to collect coins for the poor, plates used for the Seder on Passover. But we don't give them just things they recognize. We like to surprise them, too. That's the wonder of a museum."

The idea for these tours goes back to the early 1980s when Lieb first contacted Horizons for the Blind. "I asked the director, Camille Caffarelli, if she could come out and help us learn how to present the collection better," Lieb says. "We had a wonderful time, and I told her all about Jewish life and ceremonies and took her through the museum. When the tour was over she said, 'Kathy, this is all great. But you could have told me about it sitting in a room. Everything is behind glass. I can't touch anything.'"

Shortly after that "we selected objects in the collection that are tactile and interesting to touch," says Lieb. "Then Camille worked with the docents, explaining how to describe things for visually impaired people, and practicing with the docents who would be conducting the tactile tours.

"That soon suggested another possibility to me, which was that this would be appropriate for senior citizens and those in wheelchairs, some of the more frail senior citizens who really just can't stand in the galleries for an hour. So, we developed what we call 'leisure tours' so that not only people with visual impairments but also those who are in wheelchairs or unable to stand can have these experiences."

The museum has another program, Armchair Slide Tours, for seniors who are too frail to come to the museum. At the invitation of retirement homes or other facilities for older persons, docents offer a slide/lecture presentation of objects from the permanent collection. The presentation is given in all types of senior citizen retirement homes, not just in Jewish ones. "We have used this as a way of building bridges, of introducing Jewish life to non-Jews," says Lieb. "The presentation is very well received. It makes us feel wonderful to do it, and it makes a lot of friends for us." Since the volunteer docents supply their own transportation, this program operates at little or no cost to the museum.

The museum also holds occasional art exhibitions that feature the work of older adults. The work may be produced elsewhere—in nursing homes or other facilities for older people—but the museum gives these artists the opportunity to exhibit their work, and it throws a reception for them.

The museum occupies three floors within a ten-story building in downtown Chicago. Since the first floor is level with the street, access is easy for wheelchair users. A bank of elevators with braille labels connects the three levels. Wide doorways and even floors make each exhibition accessible. Within the permanent collection, all exhibition cases are viewable from a seated position. A space on the first floor that is also accessible for wheelchairs is used for viewing videos. Clearly the museum is serious about making its facilities accessible.

*The ARTiFACT CENTER recreates an archaeological dig.*

In 1991 Eunice Joffe, access consultant with the Illinois Arts Council, was asked to assess the museum. "We and the consultant felt that we were very accessible, except for deaf visitors," says Lieb. "We do not have anyone who signs." Joffe also presented a lecture to staff and volunteers on how to work with people with a variety of disabilities. In the same year the museum initiated a training session on accessibility and "we invited educators from all the Chicago museums to join us because we felt that these were important issues for all museums," Lieb says.

The lower level of the museum houses the ARTiFACT CENTER This exhibit recreates an archaeological dig as realistically as can be done inside a building. "This is probably the first archaeological dig in a museum that attempts to look like the real thing as well as offer the experience," says Susan Marcus, curator of the ARTiFACT

CENTER. "I've seen quite a number that are gridded boxes, and they are salted with artifacts and one layer deep. Ours is a mountain. It's ten feet high, thirty-two feet long, and about twelve feet deep. At the back we show the strata and have windows into the different layers. The front has eleven different trenches built into it. Each trench is from a successive layer of history and has the appropriate objects from the material culture at that particular historic moment.

"Now, when we have people with disabilities visit us, we have at least six trenches that are accessible to people who can't move up the mountain. So if you are in a wheelchair, or you have crutches, or you are visually impaired and don't really want to climb to the top, you can have the same experience digging in these trenches," says Marcus.

The dig is not just for children; it's for everybody—but children love it, including children in wheelchairs, and learning and developmentally disabled children. "That's because it's so physical; there's a lot of learning that goes on simply by doing," says Marcus. "And children with severe problems do pretty well here because there is no failure. Everybody always finds something.

"When the children uncover the artifacts and objects that are in here, they document what they find. They map it, and they analyze their findings. It's the whole process of an archaeological dig without the lab work. We are very forthright. We say, 'This is a model; it's not the real thing. So instead of sending your finds off to the lab where they would be identified and weighed and sorted, you're going to bury them again for the next group that comes along.' And they do. They often bury them according to their maps. And they clean up their work space.

"With learning disabled kids, we make adjustments. If they have a hard time recording things, they'll do a good job drawing. If they have a hard time with the drawing, we find something else, like letting them dictate into an audiocassete recorder. We find a way so that everybody succeeds."

The youngsters, usually sixth-graders, dig for artifacts—some real, some copies of objects in the collection. The real artifacts are potsherds, broken fragments of pottery, that are about 2,000 years old. "They have been here quite a while. Nobody ever walks with them," says Marcus. Items copied from the collection include a 3,000-year-old canteen with a built-in cup, oil lamps, spearheads and arrowheads, and a Greek helmet from the time of Alexander the Great. "We had an artist create a wonderful copy of a helmet with a nose protector. Uncovering it is a thrill," says Marcus. "It's a beautiful piece and everybody loves it."

The ARTIFACT CENTER also features a marketplace where each of the four booths teaches something about life in ancient Israel—trade and travel; pottery and the uses of clay; writing systems of antiquity; and armaments, amulets, and adornments.

It's all hands-on and meant to be fun. "The trade and travel booth," says Marcus, "is a game. There are samples of products that were bought and sold 3,000 year ago that people still use today—spices, wool, flax, cereals, resins. The game concerns the products that were traded and the major cities where they were traded. And the object of the game—well, just like today, you win if you're the richest trader."

The writing booth has a variety of activities to teach children how to write in ancient script. They can find their initials on a chart and then go across the chart and find how they would write a sign for the same sound in an alphabet that was used 2,800 years ago. Youngsters who are visually impaired can trace the cuneiform symbols and pictographic writing with their fingers and read the braille labels.

The ARTIFACT CENTER has been open since March 1989. Susan Marcus did not at first anticipate how popular it would be with disabled children. "We soon learned something really wonderful—that we were a natural. A lot of what we have in the ARTIFACT CENTER is very tangible, very concrete, and you can learn a great deal from touching and associating. So the kids get a lot out of their visits to the center, but it's not all one-sided; we learn from them, too. They tell me things I'd miss otherwise— the shape and feel and temperature of an object, for example. It gives you a different perspective."

# PART TWO

# Innovative Programs

# Aquarium of the Americas

## NEW ORLEANS, LOUISIANA

*A*mother, two preschoolers, and a toddler in a stroller view with rapt attention the stunning Gulf of Mexico exhibit in the Aquarium of the Americas in New Orleans. The children are all fascinated by their closeness to the sharks and the uninterrupted panorama of sea life before them. What is unusual about the scene is that the mother does not have to pick up any of the children so that they can see the exhibit. Instead, an expanse of glass thirty-seven feet wide and thirteen inches thick runs from the ceiling to the floor. There are no barriers to look over to see what is in the tank. Extending the glass all the way to the floor (thus eliminating a twenty-seven inch proposed sill from the design) was the idea of the committee for special populations, which envisioned easier viewing for people in wheelchairs.

"It just goes to show," says Charles Tubre, chairman of the committee, "that as a by-product of designing for special populations, we have made it an enhanced experience for all people."

It also shows what can be accomplished when a committee for special populations is brought into the design and planning of a public building. "We were able to imbue the project developers and managers with the philosophy of accessibility before there was even a first drawing," says Tubre. Creating open access "was an integral part of the planning process—from the designing of the building, to the training of the staff, to the philosophy of employment."

Clyde Butler, first vice president for operations and construction, concurs. When the $40 million aquarium was proposed, residents voted to support the project by authorizing the sale of $25 million in bonds. Then, the Audubon Institute, which operates the facility, solicited another $15 million from the public sector. "One of our

*Visitors see four exhibits replicating natural aquatic habitats.*

*The Aquarium of the Americas, on the banks of the Mississippi River.*

pledges to the community," says Butler, "was to make this a facility that every person in the state of Louisiana could be proud of, a world-class aquarium that would be accessible to everyone."

The aim of the aquarium is not just to enclose interesting fish in glass tanks but to recreate specific environments, and it tries to bring visitors into close contact with these environments and their aquatic life. Four major exhibits are replicas of natural habitats: a Caribbean Reef, the Amazon Rainforest, the Mississippi River Delta, and the Gulf of Mexico.

Starting the committee to make the aquarium accessible to everyone was the idea of Dr. Molly Alarcon, a special education clinician and the committee's only member without a disability. Looking for representatives of the different disability groups, Alarcon first called Gerald and Ida Mialaret, former teachers and parents of an autistic child. They introduced her to Charles Tubre, from the staff of the Louisiana Department of Public Health, who had wide experience consulting with architects to make buildings accessible. Other members were added: Dr. Robert McLean, a mathematician who is blind, and James Forstall, state coordinator for the deaf who is deaf himself. "Each member brought to this project a lot of experience and a lot of technical knowledge concerning special population needs," says Tubre. "But it was to the credit of Ronald Forman, president and chief executive officer of the Audubon Institute, and to the architects that they took advantage of it."

Designing with accessibility in mind was also a good idea, says Molly Alarcon, from an economic point of view. "One of New Orleans's main industries is tourism. Here was this wonderful aquarium going up in an ideal location—right in the French quarter on the Mississippi River—and it was being marketed as another reason to come to New Orleans. Now, when you start getting into marketing, it's not just the nice thing to do to help out the poor handicapped people. It's economically smart.

"For one thing, when you make adjustments for individuals with disabilities, these adjustments are going to be very good for a lot of other people—for senior citizens, for example. With age, we all lose our vision and our hearing and our mobility to some degree. And to mothers with toddlers or kids in strollers" such accessibility enables both the children and the parents to enjoy the exhibits.

The director and the staff made efforts to involve the community, especially the disabled community. "We took our show on the road," says Clyde Butler. "We did a series of town meetings where we went out as a committee to meet with other members of the handicapped community and let them know what was going on and to say, 'Look, tell us how to make this building suit your needs.'"

By the time the aquarium opened in September 1990, the committee had been together for more than three years, working about sixteen hours a month. In the beginning they worked with the architects and the blueprints. "It wasn't as if someone said, 'Come on in and take all the candy you want,'" says Tubre. "It was, 'We welcome you to the table.' It was never adversarial. When we had differences, we worked them out like professionals and arrived at a middle ground."

When the skeleton of the new building was up, the committee held a walk-through. Then it began working with the director of exhibits. They inspected all the scaled models. The committee sent letters to groups representing disabled people and asked them to meet one night and go through the exhibit models. "That was a crucial meeting," says Molly Alarcon, "because that night one of the disabled vets identified a problem in the safety plan. 'If you have a fire, how are you going to get the people in wheelchairs down from the second floor?' he asked. 'You have blinking lights for the deaf person; you have a siren for blind people. But what do you do with people in wheelchairs?' As a result of this meeting, the staff developed a special procedure for them." The procedure involves directing persons in wheelchairs to the second-floor balcony. Here, presumably they would be safe but easily could be evacuated by the fire department, if necessary.

Clyde Butler, who, as director of construction, was responsible for implementing all the agreed-upon modifications recommended by the special populations committee, is enthusiastic about the innovations that help disabled individuals enjoy and participate in the aquarium's offerings.

"We have several pieces of what we call interactive graphics, where you manipulate a piece of equipment with a push button or a lever, which anybody can operate because it takes very little strength in your hands. For example, in the Gulf of Mexico and Caribbean Reef exhibits, there is a mounted camera. You press a lever to control it. The camera moves on a rod across the length of the tank and does a 180 degree pan, so that it can cover from the top to the bottom of the water. When you want to take a close look at something, you simply hit the zoom button, and then TV monitors mounted on the wall pick it up so that everyone can see what the camera sees. . . . the kids love it."

The aquarium is experimenting with two types of levers, says Butler. "One is thumb-lever action, which is like a small joy stick. It doesn't take much finger pressure at all to operate it. The other is a button; it's like ringing a doorbell. We're trying to see which system is received better."

In addition to making the 500,000-gallon Gulf of Mexico exhibit visible from floor to ceiling, the aquarium has made sure that, in its smaller exhibits, no surface that the public comes in contact with is higher than twenty-one inches from the floor. "That means," says Butler, "that a person in a wheelchair will not have to have special provisions to roll up to an exhibit and do what everyone else is doing. For example, youngsters can put their hands into the touch pool and pick up a starfish or a spineless lobster and hold it in their hands and watch it crawl up their fingers. They do not have to have someone pick them up and hang them over the pool. It takes the indignity out of coming to the aquarium."

For hearing-impaired visitors, every one of the aquarium's twenty-two video exhibits is captioned. They cover such topics as how fish move, the life cycle of a shark, and the differences between tropical and subtropical penguins.

The aquarium also has the services of three sign-language interpreters. One of these is a museum volunteer; the others are made available by the state for one day a month. James Forstall, a member of the special populations committee and state coordinator for the deaf, publishes a monthly newsletter, which publicizes the dates and times when interpreters are available. This information enables groups wishing guided tours to make arrangements for them.

Because the aquarium has a cadre of 800 volunteers, any group that wants a

*The aquarium encourages hands-on activity in some exhibits.*

AQUARIUM OF THE AMERICAS

guided tour can make that wish known when it purchases tickets, and a guide will be waiting when the group arrives. Tickets are sold by time slots so that the aquarium is never overcrowded and traffic moves easily. "Wheelchairs take more time and space," says Butler, "so we group them in smaller segments when there are fewer people in the building. We always know how many tickets we have sold for every hour, and we are very sensitive about not putting too many people in the building at the same time we've got wheelchairs."

"I had someone ask me, 'Why would a blind person want to go to the aquarium?'" says Molly Alarcon. "Well, the same reason anyone else would want to go—to experience the fish and the feeling and the sounds and the sights—the sights being mental images." To help create those mental images, the aquarium is working on an audiocassette especially for those with visual impairments.

"There are some important things to remember when you describe things to blind people. For example, for a sighted person you might say, 'Look at the big fish.' For a blind person, you might say, 'This tank has fish in it that are as big as your hand.' We are developing a script for an auditory guide to the facility that will give blind persons not only the background and technical information about each exhibit but also the the types of descriptions that are meaningful to them. The cassette will give them more freedom in exploring the aquarium."

The Aquarium of the Americas is high-tech throughout, including the restrooms. "Everything is electronic," says Butler. "You don't push or touch anything. You walk up to the fountain to wash your hands, and the water comes on. You finish using the urinal, and it automatically flushes. Every stall is designed for disabled persons—and so is every water fountain and every telephone. I figure that it's a minor inconvenience for the able bodied to bend over just a little bit more."

Calculating the costs for this type of accessibility is difficult. Charles Tubre says, "As a rule of thumb, to design a building to accommodate persons with special needs adds one percent to the cost of new construction. But the aquarium managers went well beyond the minimum requirements." Clyde Butler says that the extra cost of such special features as the floor-to-ceiling glass in the Gulf exhibit is about fourteen percent. "But," he says, "it's worth it. And once these things are in place, the cost of maintenance is very slight." Molly Alarcon says, "Building in accessibility saves money—not only because you do not have to do it over again but because it makes it a better facility for everybody and in the long run is very cost-effective."

The architectural barriers may be eliminated, but the committee does not regard its work as finished. "Everyone thinks, 'Well, the doors are wide, the ramps are sloped, the signage is good. This is wonderful.' And, indeed, it is. But we still have a ways to go."

One area of concern is hiring practices. The aquarium already has two autistic individuals working there, yet everyone agrees that the disabled community is not yet well represented on the staff. The goal is to have disabled persons in managerial positions.

The committee also focuses on training. "You can have the greatest facility, the most accessible architecture in the world and if your staff is not trained, and your volunteers are not trained, and the people who run the museum shop are not trained to have an accepting attitude, then you're undoing what you've accomplished," says Alarcon. The committee is writing part of the training manual for volunteers and arranging training sessions for staff and volunteers.

The emphasis is on breaking down attitudinal barriers. "The committee wants to get away from some of the old terminology," says Clyde Butler. "For example, the word 'handicapped' is not much used anymore because 'disabled' is better. It means you aren't regarded as handicapped but as someone who is disabled from doing certain things."

Training for volunteers is designed to give them the tools they need to be comfortable in communicating with persons with special needs. Full-day training sessions are held twice a year with one hour of the day devoted to the needs of special populations. At the first training session, volunteers heard a representative of the Epilepsy Foundation describe what to do if someone had a seizure. The volunteers performed some role-playing with a sight-impaired person and learned how to use the aquarium's TT. They also learned that it is always right to offer assistance and that they should never be insulted if the response is, "No, thanks, I'm doing fine."

Clyde Butler is justly proud of the aquarium's accessibility and strong in his praise for the special populations committee, but he adds, "I don't want you to think this was easy. We went through a lot of discussions and held a lot of meetings. Sometimes we impassed and did nothing. There were difficult issues to resolve." Charles Tubre agrees that there was "give and take," but he points out one very good reason why management and the committee worked together so effectively: "We had a common goal—to make this a world-class structure that would accommodate all visitors—and we never lost sight of it."

# The Bloedel Reserve

## Bainbridge Island, Washington

eople are not set apart from the rest of nature—they are just members of that incredibly diverse population of the universe, members that nature can do without but who cannot do without nature. So wrote Prentice Bloedel in 1980 regarding his decision to create a nature reserve of his estate on Bainbridge Island, Washington. He sought to create a reserve where all people could come to "enjoy and learn from the emotional and esthetic experiences of nature."

Bloedel and his wife Virginia purchased the estate in 1951. This 150 acre reserve is on the northern tip of the island in the Puget Sound. To the east is Seattle and, beyond that, the Cascades; to the west are the Olympic Peaks. A French country house stands on a bluff overlooking Port Madison Bay near Agate Pass. Here the Bloedels found "plants and colonies of fragile woodland species, mosses, ferns, a world of incomparable diversity." The Bloedels left some eighty-four acres in second-growth forest. They added trails to make these areas more accessible. On the other acres they developed various gardens, ponds, bird refuges, glens, and meadows. These are altered landscapes, but they have been changed in ways consistent with the Bloedels' philosophy that people should be trustees of their environment and not conquerors of it.

In 1974, with the idea of turning all of this over to the public, Bloedel established a nonprofit foundation, the Arbor Fund, to administer the reserve and an endowment to assure its perpetual maintenance. In 1986 the main house was remodeled to create a visitors' center. Public rooms are on the main floor and offices are upstairs. A new building erected at the entrance serves as a gatehouse and orientation center. A planning firm developed a main circulation route through the reserve that would

*Many of the Bloedel Reserve's trails are wheelchair accessible.*

THE ACCESSIBLE MUSEUM

66

not only be easy for the public to follow but also adhere to Mr. Bloedel's wishes that the landscapes of the reserve be revealed in a sequence that would show their unity and integrity.

When the Bloedel Reserve was opened to the public in October 1988, its staff made a commitment to make the reserve accessible. With the appointment of Patricia M. Ostenson as program coordinator, the reserve gained an expert who had organized programs at the Seattle Aquarium for special populations, conducted workshops on accessibility, and served on national panels on accessibility issues.

Work on accessibility began at once. With only $500 Ostenson installed a TT (Telephone Text for hearing impaired people) and paid for the printing of "Accessibility at the Bloedel Reserve," a handbook for staff and volunteers. The handbook, which Ostenson wrote with input from the Washington Library for the Blind and other groups, is a model of common sense and sensitivity on how to approach and assist disabled persons. For example, under the heading "General Approach," the handbook advises the volunteer to "Speak directly to the person, not to the interpreter." In working with visually impaired individuals, "identify yourself. Tell the person when you're approaching or leaving so they won't be startled by your presence or stranded by your absence."

With a hearing-impaired person, who may be lip-reading, the volunteer is reminded to "make sure light isn't shining into a person's eyes"; with learning-impaired persons, "give those with speech problems extra time to express themselves." The handbook is the basic training document for the reserve's fifty-four volunteers. There is one formal orientation session for volunteers, and part of it is devoted to accessibility. "From then on," says Ostenson, "it's all on-the-job experience."

For visually impaired persons—or anyone—wishing to tour the reserve without a guide, the "Self-Guiding Walking Tour" was written and produced both as a cassette and as a brochure with large, readable type.

Ostenson's experience at the Seattle Aquarium convinced her that the way to start programs for disabled persons is to work with a committee of experts—i.e., disabled persons. "It's the only way to do it because it avoids so many pitfalls."

Within a few months she had an informal committee to consult with: Mary Kimball, representing mobility impairments; Maril Elliott, representing hearing impairments; and Barrie Burkhalter, representing visual impairments. By the spring of 1991 the committee scheduled regular meetings. "We will get their suggestions on programming and ask them to monitor the grounds," says Ostenson. "They will also be

*People may use a ramp to enter the visitors' center.*

a resource for our staff and give everyone a chance to see the process work, rather than having myself always as point person."

The committee was drawn from those who were already frequent visitors to the reserve. Mary Kimball, who has used a wheelchair since having polio 46 years ago, says, "Ever since I joined the reserve three years ago, I have been kind of needling them. Whenever I saw things that I felt wouldn't be too hard to fix, I told them about it. So, they pretty soon knew me."

Far from objecting to being "needled," Ostenson took full advantage of Kimball's perspective. "When we are working on trails, I think of what Mrs. Kimball will say if we don't do it right," she says. "She has wheeled through the grounds with the maintenance staff several times, looking for places where the trails need improving and pointing out where ramps would work well, but she is very reasonable in her requests. For example, if you have access into an area and it's extremely difficult to create a circular pattern, Mrs. Kimball says it's perfectly acceptable to come out the same way you went in. It's been gratifying to us to know that's okay."

"When the reserve first opened," says Mary Kimball, "all the roads were just dirt and gravel. And that's difficult for wheelchairs. But when they announced that they were going to pave the main road, I was stunned. I hate to see a road put in. So I said, 'Oh, no, no, no. Leave it natural. Let us struggle. I can get around.' And then they did it, and now I think it's the greatest thing. It's nice for some of the older people, too. I see an older woman pushing her husband in a wheelchair or a man pushing his wife, and, you know, the chair just glides along, no struggle in pushing."

The trails are not paved. They are crushed stone overlaid with bark. They are firm and packed down well. Generally they are four feet wide, have no more than a five degree grade, and have definite "shorelines"—edges that are distinctly different from other surfaces. "We built the bark up so that the trail is very readily definable," says Ostenson. When you ride or walk upon the crushed rock, the resulting sound and texture is very different from that of the bark. This enables you to know if you ever veer off the trail.

When the Kitsap Handicapped Action Committee evaluated the grounds for accessibility in 1989, it was "impressed with the steps already taken," but added two pages of suggested improvements. The reserve responded immediately. It added two ramps to make the guest house in the Japanese Garden accessible, had a ramp resurfaced, added a railing outside the visitor's center, installed a contrast strip on marble steps, and created some pull-off areas, with benches, where wheelchair users and their companions can stop and rest.

*Prentice Bloedel's home was remodeled as a visitors' center in 1986.*

Most of all, they "took to heart" the suggestion that guides be trained to conduct tours based on the ability of the visitor. "If someone in a wheelchair asks, 'Where can I go?' we recommend the easiest route—the central gardens," says Ostenson. "A more difficult tour, but do-able with a companion, is the bird refuge. The glen is too difficult unless you are athletically wonderful.

"We train the tour guides to respond to special requests or special needs. But we don't announce, 'On Tuesdays we have tours for blind persons or deaf persons.' If a group with special needs arrives, we ask them what they want to do. If we have individuals with impaired vision, we make sure to use very descriptive language. And we make sure that each person has a chance to tell the difference in the trees along the trail—the firs, cedars, and alders—by feeling both the needles and the bark, as well as the moss, rocks, seeds, and other vegetation.

"This is a useful approach with children's tours, too. Kids really benefit from good descriptive language and enjoy the tactile objects. You don't have to be blind to enjoy the feeling of moss."

Each summer Ostenson invites the Lighthouse for the Blind to bring their summer campers to the reserve for a field trip. About twenty-five deaf/blind campers arrive, each with a volunteer interpreter. By all accounts, it is a very positive experi-

*A portion of the Bloedel Reserve's 150 acres.*

ence for them. "One boy took a keen interest in the feel of the bark and the leaves," says Ostenson. "It was clear that he was interested in botany because he drew very interesting comparisons between the deciduous trees and the evergreen trees and asked good questions about whether the fir tree was really a pine. So that was a lot of fun. And Paula Hoffman, who puts the camp together, wrote later to say that many campers had commented that even if they couldn't see or hear, the experience had felt wonderful for them."

Ostenson looks forward each year to the campers and does not regard the presence of so many profoundly disabled persons in the reserve at the same time as too demanding. She credits the interpreters with doing the hard work.

For all the effort put into making the reserve accessible, however, when it comes to seventy acres of trails, steps, cliffs, ravines, and swamps, it is obvious that not every vista can be accessible to every visitor. No one is quicker to see that and accept it than Mary Kimball. "There are places I couldn't—shouldn't—go. Lovely rocky places, places there's no way a wheelchair could get through.

"My son discovered this state when he came here between college and the Vietnam War. And after that, when he came out here to live, he said, 'Mom, there are places in the world that shouldn't be accessible too easily. You shouldn't be able to drive a car there; you shouldn't even have a path for a wheelchair.' And he's right. You can't make everything accessible. But it's just miraculous how much more is accessible than there used to be. And you can see so much of the reserve that what you miss doesn't matter."

"Now, the visitors' center," she says, "is totally accessible, as it should be. You just go to the side entrance by the breezeway, and it's all ramped, and you come right in. And the doorways are all wide; its just wonderful.

"They have a bathroom that's just huge—totally accessible, and would be for someone with an attendant with them. Sometimes architects have the strangest idea of bathroom accessibility. Lots of times when they put the booths in, they make the door wide enough, but they don't make the area deep enough so you can close it behind you. But here it's just a lovely old-fashioned big bathroom."

The visitors' center is also the setting for musical performances, readings, and plays. "Oh, that's such fun," says Kimball. Invitations and notices are sent to the two thousand members. "When you get that concert notice, you just have to hit the phone as fast as you can." The events take place in the big living room during the winter and on the east lawn in the summer so that the audience has a view of the Cascades.

Some of the performances are signed. Ostenson hopes to have $1,000 more next year to increase the number of concerts that are signed. To get the word out, she relies not only on the mailings to members but also on letters and phone calls to agencies and on committee members, to make sure people with various disabilities know about these performances and the accessibility of the visitors' center. "But we don't call up and say, 'We're having something for nonhearing people. Care to come?' That's the value in just including it as one of our regular performances. It lets people know that, with just a little effort on behalf of those with disabilities, the performances, like the reserve itself, can be for everyone."

# Drayton Hall

CHARLESTON, SOUTH CAROLINA

Drayton Hall is truly a national treasure. Built between 1738 and 1742, the house is one of the finest examples of Georgian Palladian architecture in America. Through seven generations of family ownership, this National Historic Landmark has remained in virtually original condition. It is the only Ashley River plantation house to survive the Civil War intact. It has no running water, electric lights, central heating or air conditioning. Some walls still contain the original paint. Its remarkable state of preservation and its authenticity offer visitors a rare glimpse into the social and cultural history of the South.

As with some other historic buildings, though, Drayton Hall faces restrictions on the types of alterations it can make to accommodate disabled persons. In addition, Drayton Hall had a special problem of its own: The type of tour best suited to explain the site was quite unsuitable for one segment of the audience—hearing-impaired people.

As Meggett Lavin, curator of education and research, explains: "We're a different kind of site. We're not a typical house museum because we don't have furniture. We're not a ruin because we are in a lot better condition. What we do is interpret the house. We use its architecture and the landscape to shed light on the history and culture of the area, and we also introduce visitors to the philosophy of preservation. There are no exhibits and no signage in the house. This means that visitors have to learn by hearing, and that presented obvious problems for our hearing-impaired guests."

In 1986 the National Endowment for the Arts held a workshop at Drayton Hall on Access for Disabled Visitors to Historic Sites. The Drayton Hall staff responded by undertaking a project to make the tours better for hearing-impaired visitors.

*Drayton Hall opened to the public in 1977.*

The first idea was to have two simultaneous sign language interpreters take the tour with the project coordinator, Charlie McKinney, from the South Carolina Association for the Deaf. Because the tour focuses on architecture, it uses a lot of architectural terms, and "the interpreters had to finger-spell just about everything. By the end of the tour, they were exhausted," says Lavin. "We knew then that having sign language interpreters take the tours on a regular basis was not the answer.

"The written tour was the solution. But we did about five versions before we got it right. When we tried the first prototype with Charlie, he had no idea where he was supposed to be most of the time. That was when we learned that we had to be very clear about directions."

The various versions of the text were reviewed by the advisory committee, all of whom represented the hearing-impaired community. These versions were then field-tested by local hearing-impaired persons, who would take the tour and offer suggestions. Comments and suggestions were incorporated into revised drafts and tested again. The process took almost a year.

The final forty-page booklet is elegantly simple. The major sections are tabbed: Directions, Introduction, First Floor, Second Floor, Riverfront/Basement, and an addendum. Each description of a room or a facade occupies opposing pages; on the left are crisp black-and-white illustrations depicting the architectural elements and basic concepts that are discussed on the right-hand page. Architectural terms are in boldface and clearly defined. At the top of each right-hand page is a floor plan with an "x" marking the room described. The book is printed in Presentor A typeface (twelve point, with fourteen point leading) to make it easy to read.

When a hearing-impaired visitor is on the tour, the interpreter carries a copy of the written tour and shows what page they are on at each room. That way hearing-impaired visitors always know where they are in the house, even if the guide has had to change the order of the regular tour.

A small grant from the Arts Endowment and the National Trust for Historic Preservation paid for the preparation and first printing of 500 copies. The total cost for the booklet was $3,740 (preparation of the script—$500; illustrations—$250; supplies—$40; printing—$3,000). This was a bargain, by any standard.

The booklet makes an important difference for hearing-impaired visitors. Nettie Allen, a member of Self-Help for Hard of Hearing People, Inc., reports her experience: "Strategically placed at Drayton Hall's entrance gate is an easily seen sign, 'A Written Tour Is Available For Persons with Hearing Impairment. Please ask gatekeeper for information.' Following directions, I inquired of the gatekeeper

~~~~~~~~~~~~~~~~~~~~~~~~~~~~~~~~~~~~~~~~~~~~~~~~~~~~~~~~~~~~~

*One device for mastering Drayton Hall's exterior stairs.*

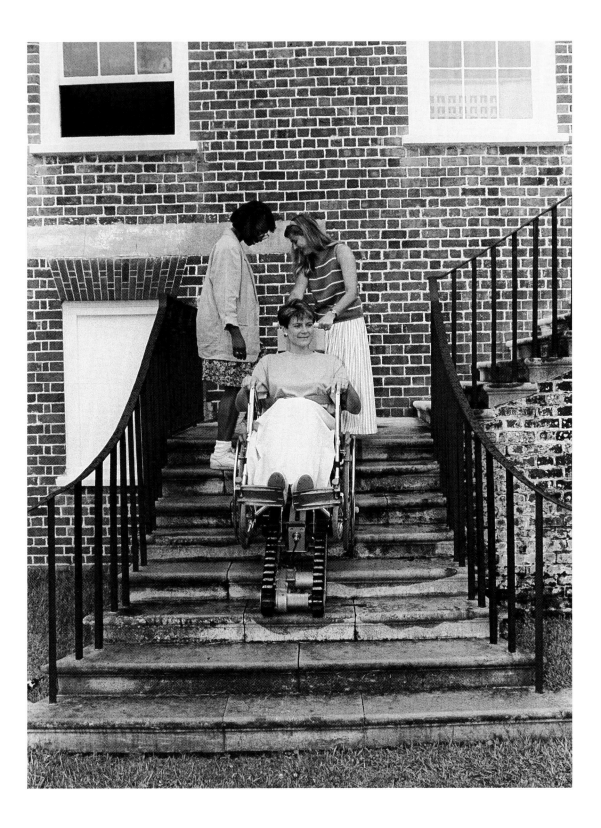

DRAYTON HALL

75

and was given a sheet with a welcome, a map of the grounds, and directions for securing and using the written tour booklet.

"Proceeding to the Preservation Shop as directed, I noted a ramp leading up to the porch and also a wheelchair-accessible fountain and restroom facilities. . . . In the shop I was immediately handed a neat, gray 8 1/2 x 11″ spiral-bound booklet.

"Since the leisurely tours are scheduled hourly, hearing-impaired visitors could have ample time at the outdoor tables and benches to peruse the booklet beforehand. . . . Its illustrations and brief, clear descriptions of design and historical notes parallel information to be given by docents.

"Being accustomed to well-furnished historical properties, I was surprised to find that the fact that the large house is unfurnished definitely adds to one's ability to more clearly observe and appreciate the architecture and the elegance of its handcrafted details. The booklet proves most effective in helping one follow docent comments and in identifying various features of the house and grounds."

In 1988, a conference of hearing-impaired persons provided what Lavin calls "the ultimate test" of the written tour. Normally, Drayton Hall staff would schedule a special tour for a group of hearing-impaired visitors and add extra museum interpreters as well as sign-language interpreters to assist with the tours. "We did have a special conference tour, but many people from the conference came here on their own, both hearing and hearing-impaired together," says Lavin. "The interpreters took everybody through on the regular tours, and it was just fine. That's when we knew the written tour worked."

The booklet is also helpful to groups other than visitors with hearing impairments. "The written tour has been very helpful for older visitors, who don't quite admit that they are hearing-impaired but do appreciate having something to follow," says Lavin.

"We also use it as a training tool for new museum interpreters. Teachers and students like it, too, because it is useful for research and pre-visit activities. Schools often purchase copies.

"We've also used it as a basis for a translated tour for our foreign visitors. We have French, German, and Spanish versions of the written tour, and we are now looking for someone to translate it into Japanese. It is a great project to undertake for the multiple benefits that come out of it—not only meeting the needs of one audience but all across the board."

Another improvement has made the tour much more meaningful for mobility-impaired visitors. Until recently, a mobility-impaired visitor could not get to the first floor. Due to damp soil conditions, Drayton Hall has a raised basement, and reaching the first floor requires going up a flight of thirteen steps. A mobility-impaired person had to be content with looking at photos, which an interpreter would explain; joining the regular tour to see the exterior of the house, the basement, the riverfront, and the grounds; and viewing the interior of the house on a videotape. Now, everyone has access to the first floor because of the installation of Stair Trac.

Stair Trac is an independent unit that lifts one person at a time up a flight of stairs without being physically attached to the building. "It was developed in Sweden and is very stable," says Lavin. "We tried it out with people before we purchased it and did a survey around the country to see how it was working. It's an investment of $3,500, but we are excited to finally have a way to get people up to the main floor."

The Stair Trac is unable to go up the second floor steps because of their angle, but even mobile visitors must go up single file to cross over a bridge that spans the ballroom out to the portico. Drayton Hall is in the midst of a two-year study of the structural stresses on the building, and few visitors are permitted access. "The tour concentrates on the exterior, basement, first floor, and landscape," says Lavin.

Drayton Hall has a full-time staff of thirteen and about twenty-seven part-time staff members and volunteers, including twelve interpreters. Most of the interpreters are paid, part-time staff members. The success of the tours depends heavily on the interpreters, who are expected to keep up with the new information that research is constantly revealing about Drayton Hall and to be expert in dealing with people as well.

The tours for visually impaired persons, for example, are one-on-one and are adapted to each individual. "Our staff is very flexible," says Lavin. "An interpreter can read the audience and do what is necessary to get across the objectives. When visually impaired visitors come, we find out what they are interested in and then adapt the tour. We have a model of the house so that they can understand the whole construction, and there are some features they can touch without causing damage. We change the tour a little to focus on construction, materials, and layout in addition to the history."

As museums go, Drayton Hall is relatively new. It has been open to the public only since 1977, but it has found ways to make disabled persons welcome and to give them tours comparable to those enjoyed by the non-disabled visitors.

"I don't think we would be very successful with a whole busload of visually impaired visitors, though," says Lavin. "We don't have enough models." She reflects for a moment and then adds, "I think we could do it in the future, though. Nothing is impossible."

# Jim Buck Ross Mississippi Agriculture and Forestry National Agricultural Aviation Museum

JACKSON, MISSISSIPPI

The sprawling grounds of the Jim Buck Ross Mississippi Agriculture and Forestry/National Agricultural Aviation Museum present a major accessibility challenge because many of the exhibits are based on historical tradition and most are also outdoors.

This unique museum is named for the Mississippi Commissioner of Agriculture and Commerce, Jim Buck Ross. As you can guess from its name, it has exhibits on agriculture, forestry, and agricultural aviation. The objective of the museum is to preserve part of the history of the rural South—to tell, as its brochure says, "the story of Mississippi and how agriculture has shaped our heritage."

To tell that story and to preserve that heritage, the museum relies very little on exhibiting artifacts in glass-covered cases. Instead, it depends heavily on keeping alive traditions and a way of life through actual working exhibits. With its cotton gin that really runs, its sugarcane syrup-making events, its mule festivals, and its country store with penny candy for sale, the museum has captured a way of life as it was seventy years ago. It's a way of life that can now be experienced by everyone, not through books or movies but, as the brochure describes it, "up close and personal."

Established in 1983 on a thirty-nine acre site, the museum has a place for everything its name suggests—agriculture, forestry, aviation—and more. The four main areas include: (1) The Heritage Center, which has 35,000 square feet of exhibits tracing the history of agriculture and forestry in the region. Organized around the theme of transportation, the exhibits go from the water era to the rail and road eras, ending with agricultural aviation, which is represented by three crop-dusting aircraft. (2) The Fortenberry-Parkman farm, built in 1860 and restored as it was in the 1920s, a working farm where chores are performed daily. (3) Small Town, a typical 1920s

*At least twelve major events are held each year.*

village with a general store, restored church, blacksmith shop, grist mill, Masonic Lodge, cotton gin, filling station, schoolhouse, and doctor's office. (4) Forest Study Trail, which has a swinging bridge and boardwalk and is the habitat of 94 of the 136 commercial types of trees growing in Mississippi. (These are identified by name signs to assist those who come to study the environment.)

Also on the grounds are a sugarcane mill, a children's barnyard, an amphitheater, a pavilion, an arts and crafts building, and a recent addition—a building exhibiting Indian artifacts.

It is a museum with broad appeal. Older adults, who make up twenty-five percent of the audience, love it. "They like to browse and relive," says Margie FitzGerald, the museum curator. "It's a great place for that." School children love it, too, and on a single day the museum might play host to as many as 1,500 students who are blissfully unaware that they are absorbing history.

The museum is a great place, too, for people with disabilities, many of whom are also neighbors. Next door are the Mississippi School for the Deaf and the Mississippi School for the Blind. A few blocks away are the Veterans Administration Medical Center and the Mississippi Methodist Rehabilitation Center. Also in the area are the Hudspeth Retardation Center, Willowood Developmental Center, and Mississippi State Hospital. Visitors frequently come to the museum from all these places, and the museum was designed to accommodate and welcome them all.

Visitors who use wheelchairs find few obstacles to prevent them from going where they wish and seeing what they want to see. The Heritage Center is a one-level building with wide, unimpeded aisles through the exhibit area. It has a telephone, water fountain, and restrooms designed to accommodate wheelchair users. Except for the two-story cotton gin, all outside buildings have access ramps. Benches, chairs, and picnic tables serve as rest stops. A boardwalk winds through the nature trail.

For visitors who may not require wheelchairs but could use some assistance getting around, the museum has a variety of options. It can lend them a motorized wheelchair or a motorized three-wheel scooter. Or staff members will load up the two golf carts and drive guests around.

The museum offers something for everyone. Disabled or nondisabled, it's fun to watch sugarcane syrup being made and maybe get a taste of it when it is ready. For all the children, but perhaps especially for learning-impaired and visually impaired youngsters, the children's barnyard is an exciting place, with its donkey, ducks, geese, goats, sheep, and pigs; and when there is a staff member or docent around to assist, some of these animals are happy to be petted.

When visually impaired youngsters go through the museum, "we let them touch some artifacts," says FitzGerald. "Things we don't let other people touch, we'll let

*Small Town recreates life in a 1920s village.*

them reach over and feel the shape of it. They like to listen to the sounds of the museum, too, and they get a lot out of the film we have. It's a fifteen-minute film that tells them what they are going to see when they tour, and all about the history of agriculture in this part of the country."

Groups from the Mississippi State Hospital also come through the museum. "Some get more out of it than others," says FitzGerald, "but with just about everyone, something somewhere will awaken them and catch their interest."

The museum is a natural attraction for older people. Its special focus, the period of the 1920s and 1930s, is the time when most older people were growing up. Most of them prefer to tour the museum at their leisure, without guides, reminiscing and sharing experiences with their friends and families. It is not unusual to see families that span four or even five generations touring the museum together. At the Fortenberry-Parkman Farm, where work is performed pretty much as it was sixty years ago, "you hear the same comment over and over," says Margie FitzGerald: "'Thank goodness, I'm not still on the farm.'"

Staff members visit retirement homes, nursing homes, and senior citizen clubs to encourage residents to participate in activities at the museum. Sometimes they will take with them such artifacts as an old iron or a high-button shoe to stimulate their interest. Eight senior adults are active as docents, and "they make very good guides," says FitzGerald.

Senior Citizens Day, an annual event, attracts tremendous crowds. Activities include basket weaving, spinning, quilting, clogging, country music, gospel singing, blacksmith and grist-mill demonstrations, and square dancing.

The museum receives about fifty percent of its $280,000 operating budget from the state, and it also receives some contributions from local industries (the golf carts and the motorized scooter and wheelchairs were gifts); but it must make up the difference through special events. At least twelve major events are held every year, and they include some lively, crowd-pleasing activities: Scottish Heritage Day, with Highland dancing and a haggis-hurling competition; a Blue Grass Afternoon; the Crafts

*Visitors learn about farm animals.*

Tour; the County Fair; the Clown and Puppet Show; a Halloween Carnival and a Mule Festival.

One of the most popular special events, however, makes no money for the museum. There is no charge for the Very Special Arts Festival, an event that drew more than 7,000 disabled children in 1991. With 9,000 children expected to attend in 1992, the festival has been expanded to two days. This is a statewide festival coordinated by the Special Education Department of Mississippi State University at Starkville. The department head, Dr. Georgia Turnipseed, plans the special exhibits. For this special event, Dr. Turnipseed has assistance not only from her department's future teachers but also from a variety of groups from Jackson: Senior Scouts, ROTC members, and service clubs. Local college sorority and fraternity members assist in preparing exhibits and activities as well as stand by to help make the tour enjoyable for the children.

Unlike most museums, this one does not need a lot of docents. The exhibits do not require explanation. Most older individuals prefer to go through at their own pace. "They don't need someone telling them how it used to be," says Margie FitzGerald, "because they know." Groups from nearby institutions—hearing-impaired, visually impaired, or learning-impaired people—nearly always have several counselors or teachers accompanying them.

When a group does require a docent, though, one is available. Groups call in advance to make reservations, and they can put in their request for a guide at that time. When large groups of children come through, the museum will know in advance and have a number of docents on hand. If a group or individual needs a sign-language interpreter, the nearby School for the Deaf provides one.

A visit to the museum seems to be a happy experience for young and old. Margie FitzGerald tells a story that illustrates the point very well: "A group of children around eight years old had been visiting the farm and were getting ready to leave. 'Come on, honey,' I said to one girl. 'We've got to hurry. They're going to leave you here.' 'Oh,' she answered happily, 'I hope they do.'"

# The Oakland Museum

Once a month two docents, Bea Heggie and Lolly Todd, lead a group of hearing-impaired and hearing visitors on a Total Communication Tour of the Oakland Museum's most recent exhibition. The term "total communication" means that the guides speak and sign at the same time.

That is unusual in itself, but what is more unusual is the fact that the two docents have been doing these tours—which involve hours of research and painstaking preparation—virtually without interruption since the mid-1970s.

The Oakland Museum has an accessible building and a number of programs for disabled persons, but it is proudest of the work it does with hearing-impaired visitors. Of the several innovative programs in place for that population, none is quite as original as the Total Communication Tour. And none reveals quite so clearly how much difference a few dedicated docents can make in helping a museum reach a portion of the disabled population.

The program began in 1973 when the Fine Arts Museums of San Francisco started classes in sign language and sent a flyer to other Bay area museums inviting interested docents to join them. A dozen Oakland Museum docents signed up, and others joined the classes in subsequent years.

"Learning sign language is like studying any foreign language, and mastery does not come easily," says Education Coordinator Janet Hatano. The museum required that the docents reach a high level of proficiency before leading tours. "We had a committee of deaf people who did the final evaluation, to determine whether these people were fluent enough to give tours. Some were and some weren't. Our committee was very candid."

"Sign is very interesting in that it is much easier to do than to read," says Hatano.

*The fish pond features a lucite sculpture by Bruce Beasley.*

"Some docents thought they were doing it correctly, but it was difficult for the deaf people to understand them."

Those who eventually became proficient in sign went on for more intensive training at the California School for the Deaf and other schools in the area. And all of this training, at least in the beginning, was paid for by the docents themselves.

A handful of docents survived this rigorous training and went on to give tours, but over the years most dropped out. "They moved away or took jobs," says Heggie. "I'm the only one left from the original group. Lolly came in a couple of years later with another big class, and they've all dwindled away. Now it's just down to the two of us."

Two, however, is all it takes to make a difference.

Heggie and Todd give tours of the special exhibits so that hearing-impaired persons have access to them as well as the permanent exhibits. Heggie has said that "the work takes a great deal of time, a great deal of commitment," a remark which understates the case. Each month they go through the same discipline: "First we do a walk-through of the exhibition with the curator," says Heggie.

"Then we do our research and write our scripts for the tour. We sign these for the teacher, Betty Ann Prinz, a deaf person who teaches in college. She looks at the work for signing, not content. Then the curator looks at the script for accuracy." And such perfectionists are they that, after all these years, they still feel better if they practice before giving the tour.

The tour itself is not in American Sign Language (ASL) but in Signed Exact English. As Janet Hatano explains, "You can't talk while you're signing ASL, because it's two different languages. In ASL the grammar is different from English. So, there is another signed language called Signed Exact English. A number of deaf people grew up learning it. It uses a lot of ASL signs, and Bea and Lolly incorporate those signs into their presentation."

The Total Communication Tours fill a real niche in programming for hearing-impaired people. Because these tours involve both speaking and signing, they appeal to people who are becoming hearing-impaired and are learning sign language. "They want to communicate and want to learn the language; they want to join in and be part of a group," says Heggie. It's also the kind of tour that can be enjoyed by a hearing-impaired person and a hearing spouse.

The two docents have developed a loyal following. "Most of these people never had any art education, and it's interesting to see how over the years they have become interested in art and museum exhibitions," says Heggie. "In fact, recently one

*Docent Bea Heggie leads a Total Communication Tour.*

*The Gallery of California Art.*

of the group didn't like the way we were explaining something, so he turned around and explained it himself. And I thought, 'Well, we've come a long way.'"

The work Heggie and Todd do poses some questions: Why do some docents give so much time and energy? What gets them going? What keeps them going? "It's the challenge," Heggie says. "I had a deaf friend, so I was interested. And then the flyer came around announcing classes in sign, so there was the challenge. And I thought, 'Well, why not?' So, I did." She stays because the work is "stimulating" and because "there is such good camaraderie with the group."

Janet Hatano, who is in charge of training for the museum's 320 active docents, agrees. "People become docents because they want to learn something new, and they want to serve in some way. But the friendships and the special bonds that are formed keep them going." Hatano also believes that the more difficult and challenging a program is, the deeper the bonds are.

Another program for hearing-impaired visitors was an outgrowth of a 1986 special exhibition of the work of Granville Redmond, a hearing-impaired landscape artist and graduate of the California School for the Deaf. "During the exhibition we did a lot of work with the California School for the Deaf and with local organizations for the deaf, and we held a symposium and an all-day festival," says

Hatano. "Because of that, interest in the hearing-impaired community grew; and three people, all hearing-impaired, expressed interest in participating in our docent program."

Bringing them on board as docents, however, was not an easy matter, since all had to go through the standard year of docent training—and to do so, they needed professional sign interpreters during the training sessions. Eventually, the museum got funding from the California Arts Council to provide interpretation for them. All three—Stan and Marie Smith and Igor Kolombatovic—have graduated and now conduct tours in American Sign Language. "We have funding so that they can continue their full participation in the docent program and attend advanced training sessions," says Hatano. "It's worked out very well.

"It was terrific having them in the docent class," she says. "Sign language is a very expressive language, and I think the hearing docents really learned from them how to be more expressive and use gesture in interpreting a painting. I think they made real contributions to that class."

During the three months of the Granville Redmond exhibit, the museum featured opportunities for hearing-impaired students to work with hearing-impaired artists as well as tour the exhibition. The program was so successful that a version of it has been added as a regular museum offering.

At the exhibition, Igor Kolombatovic, a retired artist formerly with Chevron, helped the students understand a little more about art and work on their own art projects. "He's magic with children; he establishes rapport with them very quickly," says Hatano, "and of course he is a good role model as well. He would talk to them about what it was like to be an artist.

"He showed them his own work, which is very different from Redmonds' work. Redmonds is a tonalist and is also influenced by the Impressionists. Igor's work is loud and exciting, so there was a real color contrast and subject-matter contrast as well. So the students were able to see a variety of work by deaf artists. Then they did a painting, usually a landscape, of their own.

"Now we offer this program regularly, but it is not connected to special exhibitions. At least twice a year we will bring back Igor to work with deaf students. When he does that, he is not a volunteer docent but a paid museum teacher. Then we also work with some other deaf artists in the area in that same format.

"We will probably never do all the things we'd like to do," says Hatano, "but over the years, we feel we have strengthened and expanded our programs for deaf visitors. By continuing to involve deaf people in planning, implementing, and evaluating our programs, we hope to continually improve them."

# Winterthur Museum, Garden, and Library

Achieving true accessibility, especially in a historic setting, is likely to be especially difficult and may result in small victories. No place better illustrates the difficulties of achieving accessibility—even with the right philosophy and the right person in place—than the Winterthur Museum, Garden, and Library, located near Wilmington, Delaware.

Winterthur, the country estate of three generations of DuPonts, is located in the midst of 900 acres of rolling woodlands, meadows, and streams in the Brandywine Valley. The original twelve-room house, designed in the Greek Revival style, was built in 1839, but changes and additions have engulfed most of the original structure, though portions of the original interior architecture may still be seen.

Henry Francis DuPont, who was born in Winterthur in 1880 and always loved the place, transformed it during his lifetime from a private estate to a public museum. A lover of horticulture, he also oversaw the extensive landscaping, which combines natural landscapes with a garden of spectacular beauty.

In 1931 he added an extensive wing to the house to display his collections of American antiquities and decorative arts. To create appropriate period settings for his furniture and accessories, he purchased interior architectural elements from buildings along the Eastern seaboard. The 89,000 objects, representing the very best in American craftsmanship, are displayed in 196 room settings, which reflect life in early America from 1640 to 1860. The museum and garden have been open to the public since 1951.

The challenges (associate curator of education Valerie Coons does not speak of "problems," only of "challenges") to making all of this accessible are tremendous: Miles of paths wander through the woods and garden, often up steep hills. Virtually

*A visitor on a "touch tour" handles a silver tankard made by Paul Revere.*

everything is historic: the interior architecture, the furnishings; even such outdoor settings as the reflecting pool have architectural and historical significance.

A visit there may be, at first, discouraging to one looking primarily for accessibility. A wheelchair user who is dropped at the entrance to the visitors' pavilion must travel about twenty yards to find a curb cut. In the cafeteria and shops, high counters and narrow aisles can create difficulties for wheelchair users. Yet, the shuttle bus that runs every ten minutes from the visitors' pavilion to the museum is equipped to take a wheelchair. There is accessible parking near the museum. However, the trails through the garden are sometimes steep, including the trail designated as a wheelchair-accessible route. In the museum, some steps are too steep to be ramped, and almost everywhere the light levels are kept low to protect sensitive objects.

And yet, one gets a sense that changes are taking place at Winterthur. As recently as the early 1980s the museum still thought of disabled persons as separate, scheduling both "blind tours" and "wheelchair tours." Valerie Coons, who was a full-time staff member who spent "about seventy-five percent" of her time on accessibility issues, articulates a new approach: "Our accessibility philosophy is based on integrated programming. In other words, we avoid 'special' or separate programs for people with disabilities and do our best to enable disabled and nondisabled visitors to participate equally in the same programs."

Integrated programming is a major goal—perhaps the key goal for true accessibility. It has largely been accomplished at Winterthur. There are still rough spots with room for refinements, but the direction is clear. To take a close look at what is happening at Winterthur is to appreciate how far resourcefulness can go in meeting the challenges inherent in making historic homes accessible.

Visitors who use wheelchairs now have access to about ninety percent of the rooms. As to the nineteen or so rooms that they may miss, in many cases they can see similar items in accessible rooms; for the exceptions, photographs are often available.

The tours may involve minor inconvenience. In some rooms, space is so tight that the wheelchair user must back out the same way she came in. Routing can be circuitous. When a tour with a wheelchair user goes to a different floor, the whole group backtracks to an elevator—the museum has four, and three accommodate wheelchairs. Considering the collection that may be viewed, however, the inconvenience is undoubtedly worth the trouble.

To compensate for the low lighting, which can be especially bothersome for visually impaired visitors, some rooms contain high-contrast black-and-white pho-

*Winterthur's original Greek-Revival style building.*

WINTERTHUR MUSEUM, GARDEN, AND LIBRARY

*Winterthur is located on 900 acres in the Brandywine Valley.*

tographs. These photographs help clarify objects that cannot be seen clearly. The museum guides are also helpful. "They are trained," says Valerie Coons, "to give an overview of a room, to orient a visually impaired person to let him know where he is within the setting, to go from the larger picture to the details, selecting words that are concrete and relating descriptions to things that are familiar in size and in a person's daily life."

A large-print booklet on Winterthur's popular Two Centuries Tour is free. It can enhance the tour for visually impaired persons and, in fact, it is helpful for anyone who browses through it in advance.

On touch tours those who are blind or visually impaired may handle selected museum artifacts with supervision by the trained staff. The objects are selected for their tactile interest, historical or aesthetic significance, and educational value. Touchable objects include a Philadelphia Chippendale high chest, a silver tankard made by Paul

Revere, and a Chinese porcelain soup tureen in the shape of a duck. In addition, the Touch-It Room, used regularly for school and family programs, offers interesting tactile objects, such as a pewter spoon and its spoon mold and table legs turned with the spools and knobs common in the early eighteenth century.

Hearing-impaired visitors who make advance requests may have a certified sign-language interpreter accompany them on house or garden tours. The museum guide then presents the "regular" tour to a group that includes both hearing and hearing-impaired visitors. (The interpreter is hired especially for the occasion, and funding comes from the education division's $5,000 budget for such accessibility costs.)

Guides receive special training to work with sign-language interpreters. "It's mostly a matter of giving them guidelines about such matters as where to position themselves in relation to the interpreter and the hearing-impaired guest," says Coons. "Guides also must know how to pace themselves; they must allow the visitor time to look because a person who is watching a sign-language interpreter hasn't had time to see the objects in the room."

For a visitor with a learning or mental disability, the museum guide again adapts the tour according to the visitor's needs as she has been trained to do.

The guides, in fact, are one of the reasons that accessibility works at Winterthur. There are about ninety paid, part-time guides, and they have been thoroughly trained, not just in American decorative arts but in accessibility issues. Coons, who does accessibility training, says, "When we hire a new class of museum guides, their initial two-week training program has an accessibility component. This includes a general workshop where we discuss the philosophy behind integrated programming and try to increase general awareness of accessibility issues. We follow this with a walk-through of the tour for which they are training, where we get down to more practical matters—how to adjust for the lower light levels, how to develop verbal descriptive skills for visually impaired persons, how to work with a sign-language interpreter, how to adapt the tour content for visitors with cognitive disabilities—the real nitty-gritty.

"After several months, the guides will be trained for another tour, and again, there is an accessibility component to the training. We build on the general information they already have and apply it to the particular tour situation. It's not like having a training program every two months—it's not that regular—but it is continuous."

The guides also have access to excellent materials on disabilities and ways to assist disabled persons. Coons has gathered some of the best articles in the field and placed them in a three-ring binder as part of a continuing self-education program that guides are expected to participate in.

Although most of the paths through the gardens are paved and wide, visitors in wheelchairs might find some of them too steep to tackle independently. Tram tours through the gardens, however, are available from April through October, and one tram is equipped with a ramp and can accommodate two visitors in wheelchairs. Garden guides are also prepared to provide detailed verbal descriptions for visitors who are blind or visually impaired.

To help her "chip away" at the challenges that Winterthur still poses, Coons gathered together an advisory committee of ten people, seven of whom have disabilities. The committee helps put the museum in touch with groups of disabled persons. One advisor, for example, has been instrumental in getting members of the Delaware Association for the Blind to visit Winterthur. Another has helped open up opportunities to publish articles in a local newspaper that is geared toward access. Coons also feels that the advisory group strengthens her position: "I'm sure this is true at most institutions—recommendations from expert outsiders sometimes carry more weight than the same recommendations from staff. So, I feel I have a little more leverage when I have an advisory group behind me."

Winterthur recently completed construction of a new building with galleries for permanent and changing exhibitions that opened to the public in 1992. Coons was particularly pleased with the opportunity this gave her to "get in on the ground floor" and make accessibility a routine part of planning.

She has had some victories: there will be enough floor space around displays to accommodate wheelchair users, exhibits will be mounted so that they are visible from wheelchairs, and the exhibit will include tactile components. On her advisory committee is an architectural accessibility specialist who helps her red-flag items that do not meet accessibility codes. But there are some disappointments, too. "I'd love to have the feeling that among my co-workers there is 100 percent support for accessibility in practice as well as in theory," she says, "but that's a little unrealistic. It doesn't always click that the issue is looking at the audience as a whole and thinking of accessibility in integrated terms. But then," she acknowledges, "changing attitudes is a long-term process."

It is a process, though, that seems well underway at Winterthur.

*Winterthur was home to three generations of DuPonts.*

# PART THREE

# Broad-Based Programs

# The Metropolitan Museum of Art

NEW YORK, NEW YORK

*I*f museums had epithets in the manner of medieval kings, the Metropolitan Museum of Art's might be The Great. Unsurpassed in the excellence and scope of its collection, the scale of its building, or the size of its operating budget ($76 million), this most famous of American museums traditionally does things on a grand scale.

Certainly this is true of its services for disabled visitors. An extensive program covers everything—touch tours for visually impaired persons, tours with sign-language interpreters for hearing-impaired visitors, auditoriums equipped with infrared sound-enhancement systems, scripts of recorded tours for special exhibitions, guided tours for special education classes, workshops for special education teachers, large-print brochures. The list continues.

Instead of a superficial look at everything, however, this chapter focuses on two first-rate ideas implemented by the museum. Both are unique, and both could easily be replicated and adapted to fit the needs of smaller museums. The first is a small-scale program that was created for an underserved audience—families with developmentally disabled members. The second is an in-house accessibility committee that is structured so that it can identify problems and solve them with a minimum of delay and red tape.

"Discoveries," is the aptly named program that provides developmentally disabled persons a point of entry into the world of art. Given on Sundays throughout the school year, the two-hour workshops are built around such themes as "Tombs, Temples, and Treasures," and "Arms and Armor." Another program, "Make Yourself at Home" provides an inside look at lifestyles of long ago through exploration of period rooms.

*For special exhibitions, the Met evaluates the needs of disabled visitors.*

Parents learn about these workshops through yearly brochures that the museum produces and through the networking that occurs among parents of handicapped youngsters.

From three to five families are scheduled for each workshop, which includes a guided gallery tour, a refreshment break, and an art activity related to the theme. Upon arrival at the museum, the families are greeted, taken to a classroom, and given a brief introduction to the theme. The families are then divided into groups and given the gallery portion of the program either by the program coordinator, a program assistant, or a volunteer.

These are not your standard guided tours, where guides offer information about art objects. The guides try to get the children to talk by asking them questions about what they see. "We show a picture and ask them what they think it is," says Claudia Hanlon, the museum's former coordinator for Disabled Visitor Services. "Maybe we will talk about the shapes or colors—anything that will make them feel they can answer correctly or will get them to look more closely at the object."

Even with nonverbal children, the point is to get them involved: The guide may show pictures and ask the children to look for something similar in a painting, or she may get them to make associations: "What else is red? What else is round?" "Sometimes they just nod or point," says program assistant Deborah Jaffe, "but you know you've been understood, and they definitely do respond to art."

Jaffe says that tours of the period rooms work especially well because "the children actually enter them—it's not like looking at paintings on a wall. And it's something they can identify with because they have rooms, they have beds; they can compare what they see to their rooms, their beds. It's something that is familiar to a lot of people."

"We have some pretty amazing things here," says Hanlon, "and sometimes you can see their eyes get wider and their expressions change, and they say, 'Wow! This could be a room from a king's palace!' You can see that it has an impact on them."

The program also has an impact on the families. "A lot of these families would never think of coming to the museum with a kid with a severe developmental disability because they feel that everybody would be looking at them," says Hanlon. "But because of this program, they know the other families are the same, and they feel much more relaxed about it. Sometimes they just need to know that they can handle the experience."

Sometimes families discover that the museum can be an educational and recreational resource for them. "I never knew I could come here before," said one boy

*Tours for families with disabled children include art activities.*

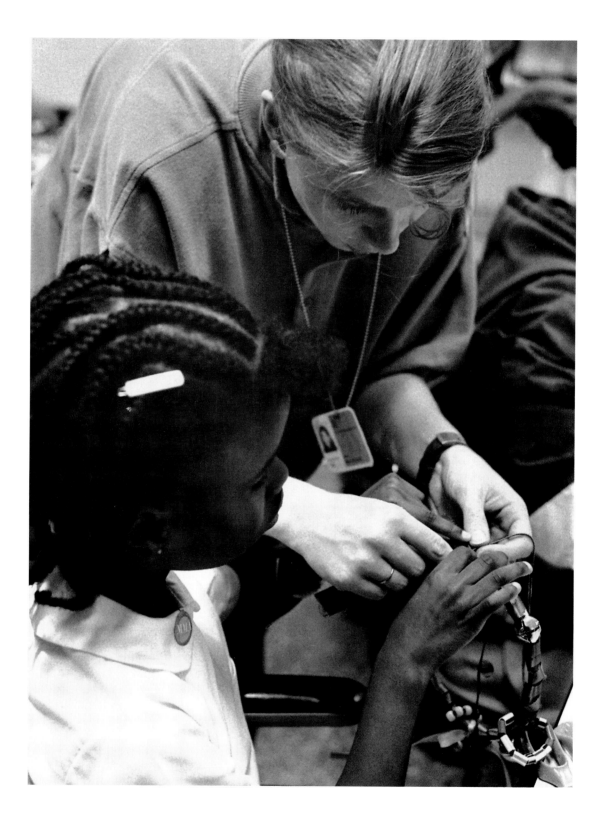

who uses a wheelchair after his first workshop. Neither he nor his family knew the museum was wheelchair-accessible.

"Often we get families who have never been here before," says Jaffe. "To get to the American wing, we have to walk through the Greek and Roman sculpture, and they are just wowed as we go through. I often say, 'There is a lot of art in this museum and we aren't going to stop and talk about all of it, but you can come back any time you want to.' At the end we give them family passes so that they can come back free."

To encourage families to continue to the museum on their own, a brochure/poster, "Five Great Ways to Explore The Metropolitan Museum of Art," describes self-guided tours built around such themes as animals, rooms, patterns, and seasons.

Back in the classroom where the children work on their art projects, "there is a lot of interaction among the kids and among their parents," says Hanlon. "On a number of occasions the parents have hooked up with each other and have helped each other with such matters as finding programs for their kids. That's a real bonus for the families—they get to meet people who are going through the same thing they are going through."

To work well, the program needs several staff people or trained docents for each workshop. For docents, Hanlon looks for "people who have a good attitude about working with disabled individuals. We like them to have some kind of experience, but even if they don't, as long as they feel positive about people with disabilities and don't view them as inferior—that's what we're looking for."

The training consists of talks from specialists on disabilities, some good video tapes, and "a lot of practice in the galleries trying different approaches," says Hanlon. "There's no magical formula for teaching developmentally disabled children. A lot of it is just being responsive to the audience, getting a sense of what the interest level is, what the ability is, and then just focusing on the ability. I think that's the bottom line in all the training that we do. It's good to know what the disability of a person is, but then you really need to focus on the ability."

The program began in 1985 with some pilot workshops. In 1987 it received funding from the New York State Office of Mental Retardation and Developmental Disabilities. It has also been supported by such private foundations as the Stella and Charles Guttman Foundation, Philip Morris Companies, Inc., and the Gannett Corporation. The cost of the fifty workshops in 1987 was $37,360, which included salaries for a part-time program coordinator and two part-time program assistants, as well as administrative expenses, publications, art supplies, and refreshments. Support

~~~~~~~~~~~~~~~~~~~~~~~~~~~~~~~~~~~~~~~~~~~~~~~~~~~~~~~~~~~~~~~~~~~~~~~~~

*A "Discoveries" program assistant helps a disabled visitor make a musical instrument.*

from the museum and the foundations is steady, but the state has cut back its funding and the number of workshops has been reduced to twenty-four a year.

The Metropolitan Museum of Art's idea of using a committee to improve accessibility is not new. Many other museums use advisory committees composed primarily of representatives from organizations for disabled persons. These committees evaluate accessibility and offer suggestions for improvement—a system that has worked well at such places as the Winterthur Museum, and the Aquarium of the Americas (see these chapters in this book). The Metropolitan Museum's committee differs in that it is composed of highly placed staff members and is designed for swift, coordinated action on accessibility matters.

The membership of the committee accounts in part for its effectiveness. "It's broadly representative," says its chair, Linden Wise, who is also the museum's secretary and counsel. "We have someone who is knowledgeable and can take action in all the areas that come into play when one is offering accessibility. We have someone in the operations and building area, who focuses on issues of architecture; the coordinator for disabled visitor services; a designer, who gets into such issues as the legibility of labels; a representative of the development office, who helps us raise funds for programs geared toward disabled visitors; the manager of public information, because getting out information is so important; a curator; and the head of the education department; and the head of human resources. The intent is to bring all the museum's resources to bear on accessibility."

The great advantage of such a committee is that it can anticipate problems and deal with them. "It's a natural trouble-shooter," says Wise. "It brings together all of these people into one room so that we don't have to attenuate the decision-making process by sending memos around and waiting for responses and having a chain of phone calls. They're all right there, and they are senior enough in their areas so that they generally can make decisions on their own."

When a special exhibition is scheduled, the committee makes sure the needs of disabled visitors are met. "We go over every component of the exhibit," says Wise "from Acoustiguides, which, of course, can't be heard by deaf visitors so we make sure there is a script that they can read, to publicity, to the route that wheelchair-bound visitors will take, to concerns about the traffic of large crowds, to being sure the labels are big enough that they can be seen and that the educational material includes large-type versions."

The committee has also initiated a project with support from the National Endowment for the Arts that will make a major contribution to the museum field—a manual of standards for the production and installation of labels in museums. "Labels are critically important," says Wise. "They are the museum's way of com-

*The façade of the Metropolitan Museum of Art.*

municating information about works of art to its visitors. This manual will provide standards that labels should adhere to with respect to typeface, type size, color contrast between type and background, lighting, manner of installation, and the material of which the label is made. The aim is to maximize legibility to all visitors, but particularly those with impaired vision, not only the partially sighted, but older persons. It will guide us in our labelling here at the Met, and we will share it with the museum community.

"That's the kind of thing the committee does best. The idea and the commitment were there, but the committee took hold of it and pushed it forward."

# Museum of Fine Arts

When Jeanne Neal heard her friends making plans to attend the Monet exhibition at Boston's Museum of Fine Arts, she didn't find it unusual that they never suggested she come along. In fact, Jeanne, who works just down the street from the museum at the National Braille Press, would have found it strange if she had been asked, since she has been blind for more than thirty years. However, when she learned that the museum was offering a special introduction and tour for visitors who were blind or visually impaired, she decided to give it a try.

At the presentation a horticulturist passed around examples of plants as he talked about Monet's gardens and the countryside the artist loved to paint. Next, a physician discussed Monet's changing vision and eventual blindness and the impact this had on him as an artist. A large-type brochure was made available to those who wanted it. Finally, Jeanne and the rest of the group went through the exhibit while listening to a taped narration on cassette.

Jeanne's reaction to the evening is best summed up in a letter she sent to Eleanor Rubin, the museum's coordinator of special services:

"'Fascinating' is too mild a word! . . . those talks we had before going to the galleries truly made Monet and his paintings come alive for me. By the time I was walking about with that excellent cassette, I felt as though I could actually know and experience each work. These last few days I've been on a sort of 'high,' and everyone who meets me—in the store, on the commuter bus, or in the subway—is entertained by my glowing accounts of the swaying, vibrant flowers and the shivering cathedral and mists over the water as portrayed by Monet. I just can't think that my sighted friends got any more from this show than I did—strange as that may sound. . . . I'm

*The museum's outreach program has been highly successful.*

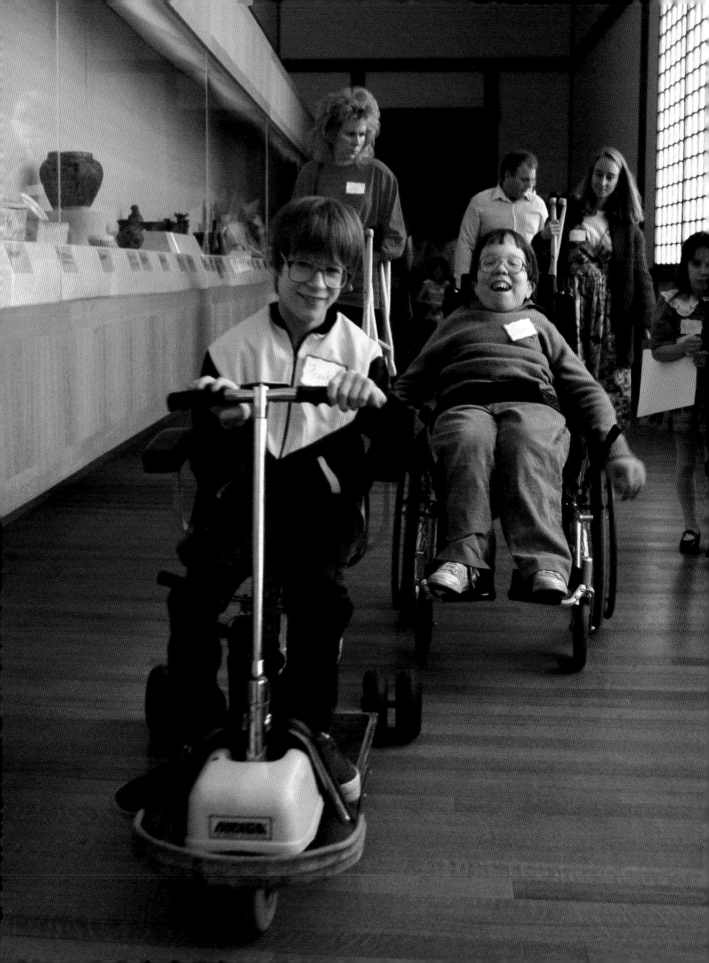

looking forward to getting back to the museum before too many more moons pass!"

This program on Monet illustrates the museum's principle that art is for everyone, regardless of age or disability. Putting this principle into practice isn't easy, nor as Rubin acknowledges, can it be done alone. Eleanor Rubin credits a great deal of the museum's success in its outreach efforts to the Special Needs Advisory Board, a twenty-member panel she began to organize almost immediately after assuming her post in 1978.

"My experience had taught me that what I needed to do was hear from the people who would be using the services and work with them to improve things," she says, noting that the board includes "a real mixture of those who are themselves disabled and those who are part of a community of service to people who are disabled," such as parents, teachers, and workers from various Boston-area institutions serving special-needs audiences. The assistance they provide has ranged from technical advice on choosing an assistive listening device for the museum's auditorium to participation in staff training.

This sort of input from the perspective of the audience being served plays a vital role in guiding her office's decisions, says Rubin. In fact, she sees the museum's accessible programming as a response to one of the disabled board members, Joan LeBrun, who said to her, "Human beings are very complex creatures. We have the ability to dream, to remember, to create, to love, and to comfort. But we, the disabled, are constantly having to prove that we are not one-dimensional. Therefore, we need to have access to institutions such as the museum so that we can share the stimulation offered there."

Physical features that allow this access include a barrier-free public entrance and galleries, a telephone device for deaf visitors, wheelchairs and wheelchair ramps, wheelchair-accessible restrooms and cafeteria, and accessible parking. In addition to these things, the museum uses large-type labels and brochures with good contrast, taped tours, and an assistive listening system previously described. All of these items have helped the museum win a special citation in the Best of Accessible Boston awards.

While these features provide crucial access to audiences who may have once been overlooked, Rubin and her staff try to go beyond simple access by actively involving disabled visitors in the collections through four main programs.

The first of these programs, Meeting Museum Masterpieces, involves outreach to people in nursing homes and senior centers by trained volunteers who are themselves older adults. After the volunteers present their overview of the museum's collections through a forty-minute slide show, the groups may schedule a follow-up visit to the museum so they can see these paintings.

The program began in 1979 as a result of a grant from the state Office of Elder Affairs to train twenty-one volunteers. Rubin recruited the volunteers from places where seniors gathered, such as public libraries. Naturally, the volunteers were not art experts, but that was not what Rubin was after. "I was very dedicated to the notion that the program could be for anyone who was interested in the arts and in learning about a museum at this point in their lives. It didn't have to be someone who had in-depth knowledge of art," she says. Eventually she gathered together a group of volunteers—mostly former teachers, professionals, and housewives in their seventies and eighties—who met about twice a month to learn about the collection and about such matters as using slide projectors, speaking to groups, and making successful presentations before being sent off in groups of two or three to facilities for seniors in the area. "Our goal was that they would be ambassadors or liaisons to older adults," teaching them something about art, but "also letting them know that the museum is comfortable, and has wheelchairs and places to sit down—that kind of thing," says Rubin.

The program proved to be a great success, both for the audiences and the volunteers. In fact, Rubin notes, "Of that original group of twenty-one, I'd say about fifteen to eighteen stayed on until they died." Many volunteers now come from the ranks of the museum's older docents. They find this program provides a way for them to continue serving the museum while being a less strenuous activity which lightens their responsibilities as they become older.

The Meeting Museum Masterpieces program has recently expanded into intergenerational activities. In 1990 it teamed up with the Stride-Rite Day Care Center, a facility that serves both older adults in need of some supervision and young children. "It's one of the most exciting things we have going," says Rubin. "Everyone benefits enormously."

Artful Adventures, the second program, is designed for children, including those who have hearing impairments or learning disabilities or are from hospital schools. The program encourages special-needs groups to explore cultural diversity through art activities involving the museum's collections from the Americas, Europe, Asia, and ancient Africa.

Museum staff members adapt each presentation to the needs of the particular audience. The staff uses posters, slides, and artists' materials to introduce the children to the variety of art they will see in the museum. The children enter into the cultures portrayed. They may enact scenes from paintings, comparing paintings in the Asian collection with similar ones in the European collection. They might use both Western and Asian art tools, or imagine themselves in a landscape painting and draw their own postcards to send home.

Susan Duncan, assistant coordinator of special services, says this type of involvement with art not only stimulates the children but also fills an educational void. "It's very important, particularly in these days when children don't get much hands-on art experience in their schools," she says. "It's one of the first things that get cut in the educational system, so for many of the kids it's one of the rare occasions when they really get to do something with art."

Another program, People and Places, introduces adults with learning and developmental disabilities to the galleries. By allowing participants to respond to paintings through such activities as sketching, storytelling, and movement, the museum staff hopes the participants will develop new or more focused skills of perceiving, exploring, reacting, and relating to what they see.

Finally, A Feeling for Form program offers visually impaired children and adults a tactile introduction to selected sculpture, furniture, and other artifacts in the museum's collections. According to Duncan, the staff often arranges these tours around a particular theme so the visitors may orient themselves more easily. For example, tours may focus on animals. "We have a number of animals that we have curatorial permission to touch in a variety of collections, so we can give a guided visit that has some coherency to begin with," Duncan says. "We can visit the Asian gallery and touch Asian lions, and then visit the classical galleries and touch a lion that is very different." Adult groups are sometimes invited to hold and investigate ancient objects from study collections and small-scale reproductions of monumental sculpture. Like the Artful Adventures tours, Feeling for Form visits for children end with hands-on activity such as sculpting animals, so that visitors have something to take home with them.

While Rubin and Duncan coordinate these four programs, they rely heavily on the approximately forty volunteers who make the programs work. Training for the volunteers, says Rubin, takes a variety of forms. For example, on-going training for the Feeling for Form group "has become a monthly noon-time event. Sometimes it's just talking among ourselves about groups that have come, and what worked well, and what didn't, and what could have been done better." On other occasions, specialists from such institutions as the Commission for the Blind visit to offer more formal guidance and to discuss such matters as "how to help a blind or visually impaired person get oriented to a sculpture, or how to describe things in terms of what somebody already knows," says Rubin. "For example, referring to a sarcophagus as 'large as a bathtub' helps the person get an overall sense of it, because touching it in one spot doesn't give you a sense of the size or the shape.

*The Evans Wing of the Paintings Galleries.*

"Some other useful things include never addressing the person's companion rather than the person—for example, not saying, 'What would she like to do today?' Also, it's important to tell a visually impaired visitor if you have to leave their side for a moment, because otherwise they might start talking to you and you wouldn't be there. That can be very embarrassing."

While these points all involve sensitivity to visually impaired visitors, Rubin emphasizes in her training that volunteers can take sensitivity too far: "It's important not to be too guarded or self-conscious," she says. "Guides should speak as they normally would and should not try to avoid saying things like, 'Over here you can see . . .' Trying to erase every reference to vision from your vocabulary is just going to make everybody feel awkward."

To enhance the training sessions, Rubin often brings in people who are disabled. "Even though I know a lot of this, it isn't the same as the volunteers hearing it from someone who is visually impaired, and being able to ask questions, and getting comfortable with that."

Rubin tries to incorporate the perspective of disabled persons in other museum events as well. For example, as part of a 1990 exhibit on New American Furniture, woodworker and furniture-maker Michael Pierschalla, who lost his hearing as a teenager but regained it through a cochlear implant, gave a tactile demonstration and tour of the exhibit for visitors with visual or hearing impairments. Rubin credits much of the success of the presentation to Pierschalla's personal experience with a disability. "Michael had lost his hearing just before college. . . . It was a very painful thing, and having gone through it himself, he has a tremendous amount of empathy for other young people who are feeling different or feeling a sense of loss," she says. Pierschalla remains connected to the museum as a member of Special Needs Advisory Board, Rubin explains.

Despite the successes, Rubin points out that obstacles still remain in the path of programming for disabled museum visitors. Most of these obstacles involve tight resources. For instance, while the museum wants to involve as many deaf visitors as possible, the cost of hiring qualified sign-language interpreters puts a strain on its budget. "I think it would be unfair to give a portrait of serving audiences who are hearing-impaired without acknowledging that the more success you have, the more expense you have. There needs to be some sort of inventive collaboration," she remarks. While she is pleased with recent laws that have given museums an added obligation to serve disabled visitors, she remarked, "I'm also very worried about how to sustain the services and not promise more than we can give."

Budgetary problems also affect efforts to integrate disabled persons into museum staffs, Rubin acknowledges. As a case in point, she cites recent difficulties her office

*"A Feeling for Form" encourages hands-on activity for visually impaired people.*

experienced in hiring sign-language interpreters and finding staff time to train a one-year intern who was deaf. "It's not simple to integrate someone who is disabled into the staff. It takes a lot of time and attention," she says. "I think it is extremely important that it begin to happen more and more, but it does take time and resources and a real commitment to do it. So, I think that while we are making laws and all that, we also really have to insist on funding and assistance for people who are making a serious effort to integrate persons with disabilities into their staffs."

The difficulties, though, apparently don't outweigh the satisfaction of working on special-needs programming. Citing the museum's emphasis on tactile contact with art, Rubin says that "somebody who is visually impaired can touch an object in one of the collections and get something that you can't quite measure but it is different from—and probably better than—any other experience he can have with that object, better than reading about it or having someone tell him about it." Similarly, she says, "visitors with emotional difficulties find something that is nourishing some part of their experience that may be at the very heart of how they relate to other people." The general public benefits as well, Rubin says, by seeing that "there's more than one way to learn something and that art is for everyone."

# Old Sturbridge Village

STURBRIDGE, MASSACHUSETTS

Old Sturbridge Village is an outdoor living history museum whose purpose is "to provide modern Americans with a deepened understanding of their own times through a personal encounter with the New England past." Through its collections, publications, and programs, Old Sturbridge Village presents the story of everyday life in a rural New England town during the years from 1790 to 1840. To present the story more vividly, it uses trained, costumed interpreters, historical farming techniques, and demonstrations of trades and crafts.

The village encompasses more than 200 acres. In the center is the village common. Houses, shops, stores, offices, and meetinghouses are clustered around it. In the outlying areas are the farms, shops, and mills vital to life in a rural New England town. These structures include a gristmill, sawmill, carding mill, blacksmith shop, cooper shop, printing shop. While some of the buildings are reconstructions, some are restored buildings brought from various sections of New England.

The problems of making the village accessible are many and complex. Accessibility at Old Sturbridge Village is a vast undertaking—very much like making a small town accessible, only harder, because it is historic; changes cannot be made that would impair its historic authenticity.

Because of the complexity of the challenge, Old Sturbridge Village has had to make a commitment to accessibility, and make it a matter of ongoing concern at every level. In 1986 the village established an advisory council, comprised of community leaders with disabilities, advocates for individuals with disabilities, and museum staff members. Their objective is to plan ways to improve access. At the same time Eric White was hired to be coordinator for access, an executive vice president,

*Visitors tour the Parsonage Garden.*

OLD STURBRIDGE VILLAGE

117

Alberta Sebolt George, was appointed to supervise the accessibility effort.

A remarkable document came out of this process. Based largely on White's evaluation of accessibility needs, "Old Sturbridge Village Access Transition Plan" details how Old Sturbridge could achieve accessibility within a designated time. This thirty-one page plan is worth examining to see why it works when similar plans often do not.

The plan lists goals with various time frames: short term, intermediate, and long term—roughly one, three, and five years. Each goal is specific and a staff member or members are designated to carry out the goal within the designated time.

One short-term goal, for example, is "to strengthen communication methods with visitors who are deaf." Three tasks are listed to help achieve this goal: "(a) continue to offer sign language interpretation on regularly scheduled dates throughout the year; (b) offer sign language classes to interested museum staff; and (c) increase publicity on sign language programs."

The plan lists the more difficult intermediate and long-term goals ("improve and stabilize village roads to facilitate visitor navigation"), and to break these goals down into doable segments ("experiment with stone aggregates to improve road surface"), and to name the person or persons responsible for getting them done. No project is too large ("strengthen physical and communication accessibility in the formal exhibits and galleries"), and none too small ("increase print size on the large entrance map.") Everything that could possibly improve accessibility seems to be included. The long-range goals emphasize maintenance schedules so that gains are not lost.

The plan works. "We are through the short-term goals and about midway through the intermediate-term ones," says White. During the first phase of the plan, Old Sturbridge Village has strengthened staff training, improved the roads, made new contacts with groups representing disabled persons, improved orientation materials, improved physical access to exhibits and public buildings, expanded sensory experiences within exhibits, improved access to the formal exhibits and galleries—and more.

In only one of the short-term goals, "to strengthen employment opportunities for persons with a disability," no recent progress has occurred. "It's economics," says White. "Going through this recessionary period, we just have not been hiring lately." He adds that "a large number of staff members do have a variety of disabilities, so we have a strong base in the past. It is just that we haven't been able to move as quickly as we would like on this issue."

This plan is an effective tool for steady progress on accessibility and not just a list of good intentions for several reasons. Strong support and commitment at the top are

*The common at the center of Old Sturbridge Village.*

OLD STURBRIDGE VILLAGE

essential. Having a coordinator for access is also key to making the process work.

What is unusual about the plan, however, is that it involves so many staff members in various projects and thus emphasizes that accessibility is everyone's concern. Finally, because the writing is clear and precise, nothing is taken for granted. Each task is specified along with the name of the person responsible for performing this task by the given completion date. All this attention to accessibility emphasizes its importance as part of the ongoing programs, not something to be taken up when other work slacks off.

Having a detailed plan, however, has not meant that work on accessibility is set in concrete. Over the past few years a philosophical change has occurred in the village's general approach to accessibility. Early on, Old Sturbridge Village was justly recognized as having developed some first-rate programs for special audiences, and it still offers some of them. Now, however, the trend is to move away from special programs for special-needs audiences.

"We began to realize not only that we were separating disabled people but we were not providing the same opportunities for all our visitors," says White. "Typically, what's good for people with disabilities tends to be good for everyone. So we decided that the best thing to do was work on providing the best program for everyone, rather than developing special programs. We still do pilot programs for special audiences, but the aim is to learn how to do something better so that we can incorporate it into our overall program."

The change has been incorporated into training. Old Sturbridge Village is fortunate in having a cadre of guides who have been with the museum for quite a while and already know how to help disabled visitors enjoy their visits to the museum. ("One good thing that comes out of a recession," says Eric White, now director of interpretation at the village, "you end up getting a fairly stable staff.")

"When we worked with outside groups . . . members of our advisory commission held panel discussions or training sessions on sensitivity awareness," says White. "Right now, though, we are on a slightly different path. We are focusing on basic communication techniques, with the idea that good interpretation is one of the keys to accessibility. In other words, what's good for disabled folks tends to be good for everybody."

Today, a guide in a typical training session would probably not be asked how to conduct a tactile tour or a tour for hearing-impaired visitors. Instead, she might be asked, "How do you interpret for a group including a fourteen-year-old boy, an adult with a hearing impairment, and a university professor?" After role-playing a successful approach, the guide might be challenged with a new twist: "All right, suppose the university professor has the hearing impairment. How do you interpret for that group?"

Despite the trend toward programs designed to accommodate everyone, at least one of Old Sturbridge Village's programs for disabled individuals merits a closer look because it has been so successful. The program, which runs every Tuesday for ten weeks, is offered twice a year to small groups of fifth- and sixth-grade children with disabilities, usually learning disabilities. At the outset each child is paired with a historic interpreter. "It's a mentor system," says White, "and a strong bond usually develops between the interpreter and the student." For the first four visits the students learn about village life—how families lived, how work was done, and what community life was like.

Then, each student performs a brief apprenticeship to become familiar with one of the trades or crafts that are demonstrated in the village—cooking over an open hearth, spinning and weaving, printing, working in the tin shop or blacksmith shop, or working in the houses, where sewing or cooking is done. Often, they will make something they can take home: "If they work at the blacksmith's shop, they will make iron trivets and things like that," says White. "If they are in the tin shop, they'll make candle holders or a box." Fitted out in historic costume, they help with activities at their work site and sometimes they assist with tours.

"The highlight," says White, "are the five days out in costume. Interpreters often say that on the first visit the children are very quiet and shy; the interpreters launch them on simple projects and spend time just walking around with them and getting to know them. By the fifth week, though, they often are interpreting to the public. They are almost in role, in a sense, and you can see a change in their confidence level."

The program culminates in a dinner where the children prepare a meal in the nineteenth-century manner for their parents, siblings, and teachers.

This program is very beneficial to the children, says White. "They have an opportunity to succeed at something, and they become the focus of attention. That's really an important thing for some of them who have never had that opportunity in the past. I think it's one of the best programs we do."

# PART FOUR

# Training Programs

## For Teachers, Staff, or Volunteers

IMPERIAL AUSTRIA

TREASURES OF
ART, ARMS & ARMOR
FROM THE STATE OF STYRIA

M.H. DE YOUNG
MEMORIAL MUSEUM
AND THE
ASIAN ART MUSEUM

MEMBERS
EXPRESS LINE

# The Fine Arts Museums of San Francisco

SAN FRANCISCO, CALIFORNIA

For Tish Brown, coordinator of the Program for Visitors with Disabilities at the Fine Arts Museums of San Francisco, it was a good news/bad news situation. The good news was that several groups of older adults with physical disabilities had come to see a temporary exhibition, and they all wanted to attend a lecture first. The bad news was that the auditorium could not accommodate so many wheelchairs.

Rather than turn anyone away, the answer seemed clear to Brown and her staff. "We actually removed thirty seats from our auditorium," she says with a laugh. "That was an interesting exercise in screwdrivers." The incident exemplifies the museums' determination to make their programs and collections available to all visitors, regardless of disability.

The two museums that make up the Fine Arts Museums of San Francisco are the M. H. de Young Memorial Museum, exhibiting American, British, and ancient art, as well as the traditional arts of Africa, Oceania, and the Americas; and the California Palace of the Legion of Honor, specializing in European art and works of art on paper.

The de Young occupies one level, and its exhibition space and entrances are free of barriers. Wheelchairs may be borrowed at the main entrance. The bathrooms are accessible to wheelchairs and contain lowered drinking fountains. There are designated parking spaces for disabled visitors in lots near the museum; and, says Brown, "we even helped persuade the city bus system to add accessible buses to our line."

The Legion is a copy of an eighteenth-century French building in which "considerable access adjustments are slowly taking place." The museum is expected to close in mid-1992 for renovations that will include making the building accessible.

*The entrance to the M. H. de Young Memorial Museum.*

Brown's goal is "to make the whole range of the permanent collections and temporary exhibitions accessible to disabled visitors." Each year some 5,000 disabled visitors and older adults participate in more than 150 activities generated by the Program for Visitors with Disabilities.

Among the accessible programming offered to disabled visitors are a wide variety of tours led by specially trained docents. One of the most ambitious programs, Docents for the Deaf, was established in 1970 by volunteers from both museums. It is a rigorous program in which docents learn sign language by working with a teacher once a week. Before joining the program, docents must have completed at least one year of study. The Docents for the Deaf include docents from several museums in the Bay Area, and the group gives a monthly tour in one of the museums. Brown feels that this program plays a vital role, but adds, "I have to say that it's difficult to maintain because volunteerism has generally dropped off, and this is a very, very demanding program."

One possible way to offset the drop in volunteerism is to begin recruiting participants while they're young, a program Brown has undertaken with a group called the Museum Ambassadors. In this program, the museums hire and train high school students from the local public school system, thereby giving the students a valuable educational opportunity and helping the museums to reflect the ethnic makeup of the community they serve. The students study one area of the collections at a time, then give presentations both at the museums and in outreach visits to convalescent homes, retirement homes, and elementary and middle-school classrooms.

Training for working with disabled students, most of whom are learning-disabled, requires extra patience and persistence, says Brown, but the results are worth it. "With these high school students, you just never know where the real stars are going to come from. I'm thinking of one young man who moved to San Francisco after a kind of rocky history. He was in special ed classes because he was hearing-impaired, and he was sort of in the middle of a new start in life. He turned out to be a star as a Museum Ambassador, in addition to being a good student. Now he's going to the University of California at Santa Cruz, which is a pretty nice thing."

The museums have also sought to enrich visits for disabled persons by providing a list of art on exhibition that blind and low-vision patrons may touch. This list, says Brown, runs the gamut "from a late Roman sarcophagus, to an enormous sixteenth-century candlestick with all sorts of human bodies carved on it, to twentieth-century sculpture, to furniture, which, interestingly, is very popular with people who are visually impaired because it has a very tactile velvet cushion on it." In addition to art on exhibition, the museums have a study collection of 500 objects primarily from Africa, Oceania, and the Americas that are brought out for any group by appointment.

*A statue adorns the pond by the museum's entrance.*

The tactile presentations of study-collection objects started as monthly programs for visually impaired visitors and were publicized only among that population. But word about them spread, and the museums, recognizing their broad appeal, made them available to all visitors, with or without disabilities.

The museums also offer art studio workshops to disabled visitors. Following a brief docent-led tour, participants work with professional artist John DeLois to make their own art based on the art they have just seen. For instance, visitors may tour a collection of American portraits, then go back to the art room and make self-portraits; or they may look at African sculpture or American folk art and then try something in the same genre.

Brown describes DeLois, whose teaching experience includes serving as artist-in-residence in a local jail, as "a wonderful artist and, above all, a fine teacher" whose

versatility in many media and adaptability to a variety of audiences have served the museum well.

"John is the sort of artist who can make third-graders with learning disabilities and people in their early twenties who are recovering from drug abuse feel equally comfortable," she says.

Naturally, adapting such projects to diverse audiences presents some challenges, but the museums try to make the activities available to even the most severely disabled visitors. For example, notes Brown, "there have been visitors who are so orthopedically disabled they can only tell their enabler where to put the paint. They can't quite move their hands to do it themselves, but that is, in fact, a valid way of making art."

The museums have produced a number of materials to help disabled visitors. A special brochure explains the programs and services available and explains which buses to take or where to park. The gallery guide is available in large print and in Braille. For major temporary exhibitions the museums generally produce an educational brochure in Braille, large print, and cassette. The Docents for the Deaf have produced a video tour of the American collection in simultaneous communication. A mailing list of 1,400 disabled individuals and organizations receives the program's annual brochure and quarterly updates.

While these programs require the combined efforts of staff members and docents alike, Brown credits much of the museums' success in serving special-needs audiences to the program's board of advisors. "I get advice from people who are experts on art and disabilities," she says, pointing out that all but one of the twelve board members have disabilities themselves and that they represent many of the Bay Area's outstanding agencies for disabled people. The San Francisco area, says Brown, "has been in the forefront of the drive for civil rights for disabled persons."

The advisors' experience in living with disabilities and helping others do the same makes them a key part of training programs at the museums. Brown recounts one recent training session in which several advisors helped docents prepare for an upcoming exhibition.

First, panel coordinator Laurie Hodas, who became disabled several years ago, explained where the difficulties for disabled visitors might be (such as a thick carpet that a wheelchair might sink into) and how they might be overcome (stand by to give the visitor a helping hand).

Next, Sandra Stone, an advisor who coordinates Youth Services at the Center for Independent Living and is herself visually impaired, talked about how docents can

*The Hearst Court exhibition gallery hosts parties and performances.*

*American art from the 1600s and 1700s on exhibit.*

assist low-vision visitors. Finally, an artist who works with developmentally disabled populations discussed art-studio projects that would relate to the exhibition and be possible for a group with those disabilities.

As advisor Laurie Hodas points out, however, the role of the advisory board extends beyond training. For instance, the panel recently completed an extensive survey of accessibility at both museums. "That took a lot of time," she says. "It involved a number of us and a lot of Saturday mornings, measuring such things as the height of paintings, sculpture, and pedestals, and the width of bathroom doors."

The efforts paid off, not only in terms of establishing priorities for the future, but in bringing immediate changes, such as improvements in bathroom facilities and a much-needed ramp entrance to the de Young's Hearst Court, an exhibition gallery where parties, performances, and receptions occur.

The ramp presented a challenge because of bureaucratic wrangling over financing. The city owns the buildings and "the ramp was on the list of things done, or could be done, but who knows when?" However, the museums' administration became so convinced of the ramp's importance, it went ahead and paid the $6,000 for it. This move Hodas sees as an example of the museums' commitment to welcoming disabled visitors. "It's been exciting," she says. "The administration has been listening to us, and that's been rewarding."

She sees this sort of commitment to disabled visitors as a plus for all visitors, since such improvements as the Hearst Court ramp aids a parent with a stroller as well as a wheelchair user, while large-print labels assist a visitor who wears bifocals as well as a visually impaired person.

"Our hope," says Laurie Hodas, "is that when people get to know us, they'll start thinking of us as being just like everybody else who enjoys coming to museums and seeing the art. That's our goal."

# Kimbell Art Museum

FORT WORTH, TEXAS

*T*he Kimbell does not look like the type of museum where one would expect an expansive education program. The museum building is a masterpiece designed by American architect Louis I. Kahn. The Kimbell has elegant, open spaces designed primarily for viewing art. Yet, the museum, which houses a small but superb collection of European, Asian, Mesoamerican, and African art, also sponsors a variety of workshops, with special emphasis on those for hearing-impaired and visually impaired children. Since the auditorium is small and there are no classrooms, most activities take place within the galleries. Tables for workshops are set up there.

Ideas for the workshops often spring from something that is going on in the galleries. When the museum exhibited modern Chinese painting, hearing-impaired children first viewed a film about Chinese brush-painting techniques. Then, they tried painting using the same methods. When the museum showed African portraits, the children made papier-mache masks and decorated them with beads and fabrics. The youngsters appear to enjoy these projects immensely, but their purpose is a serious one. "We continue to stress basic artistic concepts like line, form, and color," says education coordinator Sharon Chastain, who writes and organizes the workshops, "and we teach about other cultures."

When a typical two-hour workshop begins, the students are divided into four groups of six or seven, each with two docents and one or two sign-language interpreters. In the workshop on Islamic art, for example, the group first views a captioned film showing Islamic geometric patterns on buildings, tiles, and ceramics. Then they head for the galleries, with docents and interpreters, to study the real thing. Back in their own area, they talk about what they have seen, observing that

*A workshop for visually impaired children.*

the same patterns in various sizes are repeated on rugs, tiles, and manuscripts. On their tables are materials for hand-work: stencils in hexagonal and octagonal shapes. Using the stencils, they make their own geometric patterns, which they decorate with colored pencils.

Chastain usually breaks up the time the children spend in the galleries. "It's tiring to be looking all the time to read sign language," she says. Later, the groups will go back to the galleries to look at Islamic floral designs and then will create their own floral designs and paint them on tiles.

Preparing a workshop such as this takes a great deal of advance work, not only to prepare the materials but to make sure that all the people involved—teachers, docents, and interpreters—have the information they will need. Chastain prepares the program, including introducing the basic concept, the objects to illustrate it, the general background, and sometimes slides. Mike Cinatl, head of the Interpreting for the Deaf Program at nearby Tarrant County Junior College, looks over the material and creates a vocabulary list of basic signs.

A week before each program these materials go to both the classroom and to the docents. This gives everyone a chance to prepare, as well as a common artistic vocabulary. "One of the things you discover," says Chastain, "is that there are no signs for some of the words we use. These workshops always add words to the students' vocabulary. When there is no sign, Mike invents one. Once, for example, we had a workshop on mythology that went along with an exhibition of Greek pottery. Mike had to make up names in sign for the gods and goddesses."

Chastain also conducts a training program for the docents each month that workshops are presented. When they get new workshop material, they discuss potential problems. "You need to work things out in advance," says Chastain. "You need to know where you [physically] stand in relation to the work of art and to the interpreter. We go over ways to relate the crafts and painting sessions to what the children will see in the galleries. And we figure out how to break down the projects into small tasks because you must not rattle on. You have to give your instruction and then let them do it."

An impressive number of hours go into planning and preparing each workshop. Each workshop involves eight docents and six to eight sign-language interpreters. Most museums would have trouble finding, let alone paying for, that many sign-language interpreters for workshops on a regular basis. The coming-together of a number of lucky circumstances makes it possible for the Kimbell to have them. The interpreters are part of the Interpreting for the Deaf Program at Tarrant County Junior College, and the Kimbell Art Museum is an official practicum site. About a dozen students are assigned to the museum at the conclusion of their training. They are not

*The Kimbell is one of Louis I. Kahn's most renowned designs.*

paid; however, successful completion of the work is their last step to certification.

With the docent volunteers, the work is obviously a labor of love. "I have eight docents on the hearing-impaired workshops," says Chastain. "Most of them do it all the way through the school year, year after year. Some have been doing it since we began the pilot program in 1983. They read the literature on deaf education and develop real skills. Some also work with the vision-impaired workshops. Though that means working with an entirely different set of problems, the fact that you tailor what you do to the individual child seems to translate from one workshop to the other."

Like the interpreters, the docents are constantly evaluated. "If we see people who use their hands too much, who don't stay with the interpreters, or who don't use good facial expressions, we retrain," says Chastain. "We are always trying to improve the workshops and always learning from them."

One of the things that Chastain and the docents learned early on was not to misuse their limited knowledge of sign. All of the docents have picked up some words and expressions in sign language, and Chastain has had a semester or two of study. ("Sign is very difficult," she says. "It's like speaking French and playing the piano at the same time.") At an early workshop they greeted the students and introduced themselves in sign, thus giving the false impression that they could communicate in sign. When the youngsters realized that they could not, they were frustrated and angry.

Programs such as workshops for hearing-impaired youth take more than the luck of being located near a college that trains sign-language interpreters or the good fortune of having dedicated docents. Such programs always begin with support at the top, and so it was with the Kimbell. In the early 1980s Director Edmund Pillsbury decided to make the museum's resources accessible to every level of the community. He did not mean architecturally accessible, for the newly built museum was, of course, physically accessible from the start. Rather, he wanted programs that would reach out to the entire community.

Among the results of this policy has been the remarkable series of workshop programs. In addition to the workshops for hearing-impaired children, there are workshops for hearing-impaired adults, tours for older adults, workshops for children and their parents, and workshops for visually impaired children. All of the workshops have been innovative, but none, perhaps, has broken as much new ground as have the workshops for visually impaired youngsters.

Curator of education Marilyn Ingram, who began these workshops in 1982, wrote all around the country trying to find a model to look at before she started. "I was unable to uncover anyone who could give me a lead," she says. "But I thought it could be done. So I thought we would just try to make it work and learn as we went along."

Working with Cheryl Neely, "a wonderful teacher of visually impaired children," Ingram did, indeed, find ways to make it work. The aim was never to keep children busy with pleasant arts-and-crafts projects; it was to teach the principles of art. "I felt that they were not getting something that is important in every part of our lives— an understanding of such concepts as balance, harmony, and proportion. Without vision, it is difficult to absorb these ideas, yet they are basic to an understanding of music, literature, logic, poetry."

How do you teach balance and proportion to a group of eight-year-olds with little or no vision? Ingram began with the museum itself. A scale model of the museum introduced the children to the idea of an ordered space. Then they used their sense of touch to explore the building's symmetry and rhythms. Ingram explains: "We have

~~~~~~~~~~~~~~~~~~~~~~~~~~~~~~~~~~~~~~~~~

*"Seeing" a sculpture through touch.*

*Learning the principles of art through touch.*

very few materials—travertine, concrete, stainless steel, and wood. But the use of these materials is consistent and logical, so that the material means something when you come across it. The travertine is twenty feet across, and the wood panel is ten feet across; that's repeated across the big walls. It's a symmetrical building, and symmetry is one of the concepts it's important for them to learn—and not something they could pick up easily and intuitively."

Ingram took them into the usually off-limits study library and let them feel the vaulted ceilings. She let them touch sculptures, rejecting the usual cotton gloves as "too thick" for this purpose and purchasing for them "anatomy gloves like doctors wear." They did a landscape composition using textures. "The things up close they could feel in great detail; things farther away they could sense. So they used silks and satins for very distant things and rough textures like wool tweed and canvas for the close-up things."

They learned about structure through such activities as touching a chambered nautilus that had been cut apart so they could feel all the chambers, and building foam rubber arches large enough to walk through.

They learned about balance by using a scale, which has two trays on either side of a fulcrum. "Balance is usually a visual judgment, but it can be tested on the scales," says Chastain, who has directed the visually impaired workshops since 1989.

The good news is that these workshops work. The bad news is that the school system has cut back on expenses and has canceled field trips. (The Kimbell pays the costs of the workshops, but the schools must provide the transportation for visually impaired children.) Last year, the usual three workshops a month were cut to three a year, with only the Arlington school district participating.

It is probably helpful to be philosophical about a situation like this and to re-member how useful it is that the workshops have been done and that the model for replicating them exists.

# Lawrence Hall of Science

### Berkeley, California

*A*ll Lawrence Hall of Science programs share a similar goal: to spark curiosity and excitement about science and math," says Director Marian C. Diamond. Established in 1968 on the University of California at Berkeley campus, the Lawrence Hall of Science (LHS) is both a science museum and a research center dedicated to improving science education in the schools.

Over the years, the Lawrence Hall of Science has developed hundreds of lively programs in astronomy, biology, chemistry, earth science, mathematics, physics, and technology. Each year more than 94,000 students from kindergarten though high school explore the hall's exhibits, computer labs, and laboratory classrooms. Or they come to take workshops on such topics as Prehistoric Puzzles, Crime Lab Chemistry, Tracking Down Dinosaurs, Columbus' Environmental Impact, Is Anybody Out There? and Tin Can Cameras. Another 128,000 students in Northern California participate in the same programs when the Lawrence Hall of Science staff bring workshops and assemblies to the schools.

"Activities developed at the Lawrence Hall of Science help students learn about math and science by doing math and science," says Diamond, describing the hall's hands-on approach to education. For the purposes of the present study, what is especially noteworthy is that Lawrence Hall of Sciences has pioneered the application of this hands-on approach to science programs for disabled youngsters.

In 1976 a department of the Lawrence Hall of Science, the Center for Multisensory Learning (CML), received funding from the United States Office of Education to undertake Science Activities for the Visually Impaired (SAVI), a project designed to produce science enrichment activities for blind and visually impaired students in

*Children participate in a multisensory learning program.*

upper elementary through junior high school. Three years of developing specialized equipment and new procedures resulted in nine modules of hands-on multisensory science activities. During the extensive field testing, staff made an interesting discovery: not only did the materials work well with blind and visually impaired students, but they also worked very well for students who had other disabilities.

This revelation led to the next logical step; and with a second grant in 1979 from the United States Office of Education, the staff set out to adapt the SAVI activities for learning disabled and orthopedically disabled youngsters, and to research how hands-on science could most effectively be used with disabled students in the mainstream. The project was called Science Enrichment for Learners with Physical Handicaps (SELPH), and its products were merged with the SAVI products to produce the SAVI/SELPH program.

The nine modules include such topics as measurements (one activity is titled Take Me to Your Liter), structures of life (featuring work with seeds to understand growth), communications or the physics of sound, and kitchen interactions (experiences with such common household substances as yeast). In the module on magnetism and electricity, students handle and investigate permanent magnets, electromagnets, insulators, and conductors while building simple circuits and magnetic systems. In the environmental energy module, students make tools to put the sun and wind to work, discovering alternative energy sources as they work.

This material is taught in workshops at the Center for Multisensory Learning and made available to schools or individuals in kits. Each kit serves up to four severely disabled students at one time or up to sixteen who are able to share materials. Teacher guides, training manuals, and videos are also available. The cost for developing the programs was $970,000. The materials are available now on a cost-recovery basis.

The Center for Multisensory Learning (CML) not only developed the new materials but has trained educators to use it. With additional funding of $696,000 from the United States Office of Education, the Center for Multisensory Learning staff conducted thirty Regional Leadership Institutes around the country, twenty local teacher in-service courses on the multisensory learning techniques, and hundreds of awareness and one-day workshops. Center for Multisensory Learning also established a lending library of materials and continues to offer consultative services to educators wishing to integrate multisensory materials into their programs.

"The leadership institutes established a network of leaders around the country," says Center for Multisensory Learning Coordinator Linda De Lucchi. "We had 300 people who went through the SAVI/SELPH training over the years. So when we get a call from someone in Denver who is interested in the program, we send them information from here, but we can also tell them who in their area knows about the program. It's still an active leadership network."

The Center for Multisensory Learning was also instrumental in starting an organization called Disabled Children's Computer Group (DCCG), whose purpose is to use computers to assist in mainstreaming children with disabilities. "We had a small grant in 1983 from the United States Office of Education to explore technology for visually impaired students," says De Lucchi.

"There were parents in the local community who were frustrated knowing that there might be technology that could help improve the quality of their children's lives but who did not have a place where they could try out the hardware or talk to people with similar needs. So for a while Disabled Children's Computer Group was here at Lawrence Hall of Science. We would have meetings with parents, educators, and professionals interested in the technological needs of disabled students."

The Disabled Children's Computer Group now has a computer resource center where families and teachers can come in and try new hardware and software. "Disabled kids can sit down in front of computers and try out things," says De Lucchi. "There are workshops where kids can interact with computers and find out what kinds of formats would best assist them in their schooling."

The Disabled Children's Computer Group works with youngsters with all kinds of disabilities, from learning-disabled to low-vision disabilities. There are youngsters who need other than keyboard access to computers, so the resource center has expanded keyboards and other kinds of input devices to get to the keyboard. The computer group works with children who have no oral communication, with children who cannot hold a pencil and write, with youngsters who are very bright but have cerebral palsy and can communicate in no way except through computers. For some disabled children, computers provide a method for expression that they would not otherwise have.

"The Disabled Children's Computer Group is now a separate nonprofit organization, part of the Alliance for Technology Access. Staff members at Lawrence Hall of Science still work closely with staff at the Disabled Children's Computer Group; in fact, several of us are on the board of directors."

Through its Biology Department, Lawrence Hall of Science also has innovative programs aimed at a very different audience. Science and Math Discovery Workshops for Seniors are free, two-hour workshops for retired adults interested in math or science. Each class involves hands-on activities as seniors work with simple chemistry equipment, gentle animals, and computers, and visit the planet Mars via a planetarium.

A more ambitious program, with serious implications for elementary education, is the intergenerational Youth and Seniors: Science Discovery Workshops. Here older volunteers are trained by Lawrence Hall of Science staff to present science workshops to elementary and junior-high students.

The workshops "address some of the major problems elementary school teachers have in making science and math acceptable to all the children," says Kathy Barrett, director of the biology education department. "When we train the teachers, we have them working in a group, so a team goes into the classroom. Providing a team of four to seven seniors who are knowledgeable in the activities enables small groups of children to have individual attention.

"You can foster cooperative learning experiences, something that is hard for a teacher to do when she is the only teacher in a class of second or third graders. But the payoff is that there is more time spent in discussing and analyzing and extending the experience because the kids get to share more of their findings, their ideas. So having a team of educators going into the elementary level is extremely valuable."

These workshops take place once a week at participating schools, and Barrett prefers that they run "at least four weeks because there is a bonding that takes place with the seniors." Classroom teachers report that their students look forward to each visit of the older adults and talk about the science activities long after the visits.

To volunteer for the program, older individuals do not need to have a scientific background. "We find that an openness to exploring with the children is far better than an in-depth science background," says Barrett. "In fact, we have to help scientists overcome their tendency to tell everything they know, which can be a real turn-off for young children." Older people are trained to "help the children make their own observations, collect their own data, write down what they have found, and then talk about what it all means."

The older docents have three two-hour training sessions, where they go through the activities they will do with the children. "If it's finger-printing," says Barrett, "they will explore all kinds of prints that can be made by things—surfaces of oranges, dominoes, pennies, elbows—and they learn how to take fingerprints of people and categorize different kinds of prints. Then they discuss the activity as a group and find out from people who have done it before what kinds of questions to expect from the children."

A number of the workshops involve animals, says Barrett, "because children in urban situations have so few experiences with a variety of animals. One of our activities has always been terrariums—putting in little pill bugs and crickets and earthworms and things like that.

"Another popular series comes from our health activities project, where fourth-grade children explore with stethoscopes their own heartbeats and compare them with guinea pigs, chinchillas, and rats. They can take the stethoscopes home and find out about the heartbeats of other kids or their families."

The intergenerational program benefits seniors as well as the students. "A camaraderie springs up among the seniors, and life-long friendships develop," reports Barrett. "Almost all the seniors who started the program have stayed with us. All of them are busy people, but they make this program a priority. It's amazing how important this is to the seniors and how important to the students."

The workshops tend to change the image children have of growing old. "Kids can have very negative attitudes about that," says Barrett. "But questionnaires we did with junior high students showed that they were very impressed by the seniors— thought that their lives were incredibly rich and that they were doing things that they wanted to do."

The program was developed in 1982 with a small grant from General Electric. The state of California has an annual line item in the budget for intergenerational programs and provides $15,000 each year for it. The program is now operational in five school districts. Each year between ten and twelve schools have the program.

Barrett believes that the program would be easiest to duplicate in places where there are museums or universities to provide the needed scientific resources and mentors but says that "in school districts that have well-developed volunteer programs, the model would also work."

# Museum of Science

*T*he teenager from the Perkins School for the Blind was getting restless, so Betty Davidson, an exhibit planner with the Museum of Science, took him over to a new activity station called "A Tool To Fit the Task." This exhibit is an array of tools paired with casts of their counterparts in the animal world—a bear's paw and a hand cultivator, a beaver skull with its chisel-like teeth and a real chisel, a swim fin and a swan's webbed foot. The purpose is to highlight adaptations that enable animals to live in their environment. "I explained the concept of it, placed his hand on the bear's claws and said, 'Now, below that you will find a garden tool that does the same thing. And that's how this goes throughout.' He felt the bear's claws, and he went right below and felt the cultivator, and you could see his face brighten. There is a look that comes over a person's face, and you know that he's got it. I started to say, 'And the next one . . .' and he cut me off. He said, 'I know what to do. Don't tell me.'

"He was so excited. No one had to walk him through and explain this activity. He could do it by himself and get the point of it. This exhibit opened something up for him. At that moment all our work seemed worthwhile."

The work Davidson refers to was an experimental project aimed at turning a gallery in the Museum of Science into a model multisensory exhibit that would appeal to and be accessible to all visitors. The process the museum followed to make this exhibit a lively and accessible place is both fascinating and probably will be instructive to others who wish to make their exhibits multisensory.

Much of the credit for getting the project started goes to Betty Davidson who has served at the museum since 1987. Because of her background—a PH.D. in biochemistry, experience as an elementary-school science resource teacher and curriculum

*The museum is located on the banks of the Charles River.*

developer, and long-standing interest in access issues—made her the right person on the right project. The museum applied for and received money from the Institute for Museum Services for an access evaluation, which Davidson coordinated.

In the evaluation and the work that followed, Davidson sought the help of people who represented the people the museum wanted to reach. Her committee included Annette Posell, director of marketing at the WGBH Caption Center, who is deaf; Ray Bloomer, disability specialist with the National Park Service, who is visually impaired; and Jan Majewski, coordinator for special education at the Smithsonian Institution. Davidson, who is mobility impaired, did the work on mobility issues. The committee did not attempt to evaluate the entire museum. They chose to look at several exhibits, a lecture/demonstration on static electricity, and the entry areas—garage, lobby, the places a visitor first encounters.

At the end of the evaluation, the museum decided to improve access to the New England Lifezones gallery. The museum applied to the National Science Foundation for funds to make this a model participatory exhibit and received $200,000, which Davidson says is "actually a modest budget."

The original New England Lifezones exhibit was an open gallery consisting of six large window dioramas and one small one. These portrayed animals in their native habitats—birds of the rocky mid-coast of Maine, beavers, a bear, a moose, a grouping of deer, and shorebirds at Crane's Beach in Massachusetts. The exhibits were explained by labels on the wall. The only interactive elements were two sets of push buttons that enabled visitors to spotlight and identify the sea birds and shore birds.

Because the exhibit was completely visual and in a dimly lit space, it was inaccessible to visitors with visual impairments. In addition, however, the bird spotlighting buttons were close together, and people with coordination problems couldn't use them; the small-print labels were hard to read at a distance and not well placed for visitors in wheelchairs. Additionally, the information on the labels was difficult for many visitors to follow.

This "was a very traditional natural history diorama. They are all over the place—big, beautiful displays behind windows, and they are explained by labels. If you can't see well, though, you might as well not be there. But it wasn't poorly done. I think that often the assumption is that you are going to experience a museum solely with your eyes. That holds true for museums being built right now."

Since the idea was not to change the dioramas but to make them accessible and meaningful to visitors—the first step involved making an inventory of the information a visitor could learn by looking at the dioramas and reading the labels. It was clear that they contained a wealth of information.

A careful look at the beaver diorama, for example, would show the size and shape of the adult and a yearling, their physical characteristics, their behavior, their habitat, and such adaptations as their chisel teeth for felling trees, the hind legs with webbed feet for swimming, the flat rudder-like tail, and the thick, waterproof fur for keeping them warm even when swimming under ice in winter.

The next step was to find out what visitors were actually learning from the dioramas. Surveys by independent evaluators showed that learning was minimal. Most visitors regarded the gallery as an attractive display of stuffed animals. Few people stayed long; nineteen percent cruised through in less than a minute. Few understood the major ideas of the exhibit—that New England has a variety of environments and that animals adapt to these environments in all types of interesting ways. Only one person in five could name one animal adaptation. In short, the exhibit was intellectually, as well as physically, inaccessible.

Staff and committee members then set some goals for what they wanted the exhibit to be and do. First, of course, they wanted everyone to enjoy the experience and get something out of it. They wanted visually impaired visitors to have some sense of what was behind the windows. They wanted visitors with other disabilities to have physical and intellectual access to the displays. And finally, they wanted all visitors to learn something about habitats and adaptations. For example, they wanted all visitors to recognize that each diorama represented a New England environment, to see that the plants and animals were typical for that environment and adapted to it. They also hoped visitors would make cross-references among the dioramas, noting, for example, that both gulls and beavers have webbed feet for swimming.

Brainstorming sessions followed. Staff and committee members suggested a wide range of ideas—from the cautious and practical to the splendidly unrealistic. "What we wanted was to bring all possibilities out on the table as a catalyst for discussion," says Davidson.

From the discussions came certain decisions: videotapes would be captioned; the exhibit would present no barriers to wheelchair users; audio tapes would be used to present label information and also to evoke as much of the environment as possible; labels would be in large print, clearly written, and well lit; there would be touchable objects. The guiding principle was that design features which allow disabled visitors to participate in an exhibit are the same ones that enhance the exhibit's interest and educational value for everyone.

"We did a lot of prototype testing—brought out new things and looked at how they were used. I called in groups to help me—from the Perkins School for the Blind, children with mobility problems from schools and rehab facilities, some deaf students in a high-school program, and emotionally and learning-disabled children from an elementary school.

Before any idea was put out in final form, I invited people, adults as well as children, to use these exhibit components and see whether they were working right. Some of the stations were modified two or three times based on the users' reactions."

In the end, two types of changes were made to the exhibit: new components were added to help explain and interpret the individual dioramas; and activity stations were installed to illustrate the common themes about habitat and adaptation.

"The new components," says Davidson, "had to help people get beyond 'Oh! A moose!' in their perceptions of the dioramas." To do that, the new additions involve as many of the visitor's senses as possible. The additions include:

■ An introductory panel for the entire exhibit. This contains background information in graphic and audio form.

■ Smell boxes. Push a button and a fan blows an odor, such as musk or spruce, associated with the scene in the diorama.

■ Audio tapes. The visitor lifts the receiver to hear an explanation of the scene and listen to environmental sounds, such as the ocean and the cries of shore birds.

■ Two-tiered labels. The most basic information is in thirty-six point print. Less important information is in twenty-eight point. The sentences are short and clearly written to accommodate visitors with limited reading ability due to profound deafness, learning disabilities, or limited English.

■ Touchable objects. The team agreed that full-scale mounts of the birds and animals in the dioramas would be ideal—a goal not possible because of the expense and the fragility of the birds and some other specimens. Instead, they decided to try full-scale mounts of a beaver and a black bear, though many worried that the specimens would be vandalized or petted to death within two weeks. Additions to the exhibit included: bronze replicas of a cormorant and a godwit (a species of shorebird). Other touchable elements included: a set of white-tailed deer antlers and the hooves of a deer and a moose, mounted together for comparison.

■ Three activity stations encourage visitors to draw comparisons about habitat and adaptations from the different dioramas: (1) Outer coverings. Touchable fur samples, which can be viewed through a microscope, show, for example, the differences in bear, beaver, and deer fur—how each is insulated and how beavers are waterproofed; (2) A tool to fit the task. Touchable animal "tools"—in this instance, specialized mouth and foot parts, are compared with human tools that have a similar structure and function; and (3) Build a beast. To show how an animal's body shape is related to the way it lives, visitors select from a variety of wooden body, head, and foot parts and assemble an animal adapted to a particular lifestyle.

The exhibit, now called New England Habitats, has been in place since early 1989, and it is possible to assess some results. One worry—that the mounts would wear out after two weeks—has been dismissed. The beaver lasted about a year and was replaced. The bear survived a year and a half—and 500,000 visitors to the gallery—before being petted bald. The replacement costs for bear and beaver were less than $2,000.

The composition of the audience has changed from mostly adults to a mixture of children and adults. The average time spent in the gallery has more than tripled.

Now, the exhibit is a lively, well-populated place. "I am happy with the way the exhibit is being used—the enthusiasm," says Davidson. "It's nice to see family groups in there with each person choosing what he or she wants to get out of the exhibit. A little child may run around and feel the bear and smell the smells and rush back to grab an older sibling and bring him over and say, 'Is that what bears smell like?' The parents may go through and read the labels to the children because that's what parents do. And somehow, all together, the sum of learning is so much greater because people share what they learn with one another within a group. That to me is very exciting.

"The important thing, though, is that this exhibit is now not only usable for a much larger proportion of disabled people but much more usable and enjoyable for everyone. That doesn't surprise me.

"What does surprise me is how the exhibit has dramatically improved how much people learn. In the beginning, maybe twenty percent could name one adaptation. At the end of this project, one hundred percent of the visitors could name one adaptation, and ninety percent could name two.

"You're reaching everybody by providing different modalities of learning. They can experience it by smelling, feeling, listening; they don't have to read if they don't want to or can't. The multisensory approach is a very valuable one. It doesn't have to be elaborate, but it's important to give people choices of how they access the information."

Though the exhibit is now much more usable for disabled persons, Davidson says, "You are not going to have perfection, even in a brand-new exhibit. You're not going to have every inch of it accessible to every human being—it just can't be done. The important thing is to make people feel welcome and to give them a meaningful experience. There are lots of ways you can do a great deal without having a perfectly and universally accessible facility. People should not be intimidated thinking that's what they need to have. They must be aware and be welcoming and do what they can."

# University Museum / Southern Illinois University

e said we were receptive to working with people with any type of disability and agreed to give it a try," says Lorilee Huffman, describing the start of an innovative program that uses the museum as a training ground for disabled people.

The program began in 1986 when Huffman, who is curator of collections in the University Museum of Southern Illinois University, met with staff from the Evaluation Development Center (EDC), which specializes in rehabilitating disabled people. "EDC was looking for jobs requiring higher-level skills for people with disabilities," says Huffman. "They felt that libraries and museums might offer some opportunities. They said they can always get their clients into places like McDonald's to clean up, but no one wants to give them a chance to do something better. This is what we try to do."

Southern Illinois University is a good place to give a program like this a try, according to Huffman. The campus is very accessible for disabled persons—"something the university takes pride in"—and it draws a lot of disabled students. It has a strong department of rehabilitation and a number of disabled student services, such as readers, wheelchairs for rent, and good support groups.

Before the first disabled people showed up to work, however, both the museum and EDC did mammoth preparation. Huffman's first step was to identify the jobs that might be suitable for training disabled workers. Talking with staff, she first did a thorough study of the variety of tasks performed in the museum. This study became the basis for job descriptions, each with its list of duties and responsibilities. From there it was possible to identify which jobs would be suitable for a six-week training program for disabled individuals.

*SIU's University Museum trains disabled people for skilled jobs.*

*The SIU campus is highly accessible.*

These included: preparing collection information on the computer; conducting research on exhibits; assisting in the installation of exhibits; assisting in collection inventory; working with the extensive slide library files; overseeing and managing shop tools; updating the learning kits; giving guided tours to museum visitors; researching and writing biographical information on artists in the collection; performing general research; acting as a gallery guard; and working as a receptionist.

Many of these tasks are the same ones performed by college students, who work in the museum as part of their undergraduate or graduate work in museum studies. The college students and the disabled staff sometimes end up working side by side doing inventories or making computer data sheets.

EDC prepares and evaluates their clients before recommending them to the museum. They generally come from the southern Illinois counties and range in age from eighteen to fifty-five. Some have emotional disabilities, and some physical; some were born with their disabilities while others acquired them, often in accidents. EDC uses what Huffman terms "a holistic method of rehabilitation." Many of its clients live in a facility on campus while taking classes in social skills and independent living. Later they may move to a semi-independent living center, where there are fewer restrictions. Throughout, EDC continues to work with them, helping them with the problems of independent living and giving vocational training and counseling. Some clients receive a small stipend from EDC through the Illinois Department of Rehabilitation.

When EDC feels that it has someone who would fit into the museum workplace, Huffman meets with the individual and with representatives from EDC. "It is all done in a very professional manner," she says. "EDC makes clients bring in a resume, and we discuss which job might suit them best. We have never turned anybody down. I'm going to give everybody a chance. I'm not going to say, 'I don't think this person will work out.'"

Nearly always they do work out. Since the program started in 1986, the museum has trained thirty people with disabilities. Of these, only one person did not work out, and EDC later decided that the individual was immature and not ready for work.

All the rest completed the job training with some degree of success. One woman who has cerebral palsy started out in the program three years ago and now volunteers at the museum ten hours a week. She has a B.A. in history and an interest in museum work. "She works primarily with the collection records. We are doing a lot of inventory, and we bring the inventory materials to her—the shelf is too high for her to reach them. But that's all we need to do for her. She looks them over and completes the computer data sheets on them. She likes doing it. She can see how much she has done to update our inventory and records, and I think the accomplishment brings her satisfaction. For us, it's like having a quarter-time staff person."

Another woman, who uses a wheelchair, went through the EDC program and the museum training. "We kept increasing her workload and her responsibility," says Huffman, "we couldn't keep her busy enough." Later she decided to enroll in the university as a full-time student and is now seeking a degree in rehabilitation.

Normally the museum staff trains the individual. Since each person works about ten hours a week, the training at first occupies the staff member about twelve hours a week since the staffer must prepare. After a few weeks they begin to work more independently on the job. "It isn't one-on-one all the time," says Huffman. "We check their work, and we are there for support." The museum never takes more than two clients at one time.

The staff does not find its role in training burdensome, says Huffman. One reason is that she brings them into the planning process, seeking their advice on where the new person might be placed. "Also," she says, "this project is interesting. It's rewarding for the clients and for people at the museum, too. We all learn from each other."

On those occasions when the new person does not seem to be working out at the job, Huffman takes a very flexible approach. "If it doesn't work, we don't get all excited. Sometimes it is just that we have not matched the right job to the person. We evaluate the person every week, so if we notice a problem, we all get right on it. We consult with EDC, and maybe we will boost the amount of training, or find a new strategy for training them in the same job but approaching it in a different way. Then, we've had cases where we just had to move them to something else. But we always find a spot for them.

"Everything depends upon the individual," she says. "Each one is unique. You can't say, 'Well, this person has cerebral palsy, so she will be like this.' That's not true. They are as varied as everyone else. Some are very mature in their judgment; others may be insecure because of their disability and fear of failure. And maybe people have always given them problems because of their disability. We try to put them at ease. 'If you mess up,' we say, 'don't worry about it. We can fix it. Everything is fixable.'"

At first Huffman was "a little apprehensive" about evaluating the clients because "you want to be kind. But you have to be as objective as you can because you are benefiting them by doing that. If you say, 'Oh, you're doing a good job,' and they really are not, you undermine the whole program."

For museums considering a training program for disabled persons, Huffman advises doing a lot of groundwork. "Most important, you need to set the program up right by working with someone, or some institution, that knows about rehabilitation. Doing it on your own without any background in rehab could be pretty frustrating, I'd think."

No doubt it is also an asset to have someone with Huffman's enthusiasm and dedication involved in making the program work. "It is my focus," she says, "and has been for many years."

Right now she is looking into ways that the program at Southern Illinois University might be expanded. One hope is to get grant support so that the museum could provide stipends and thus extend the training for a longer period of time. She would also like to do some pilot studies to encourage other museums to undertake similar training. The field has barely been explored, she feels, and it has "vast potential," both for disabled persons and for museums.

~~~~~~~~~~~~~~~~~~~~~~~~~~~~~~~~~~~~~~~~~~~~

*One of SIU's retrained clerical workers.*

# Bibliography

*Books, reports, and guides*

Allen, Anne, and George Allen. *Everyone Can Win: Opportunities and Programs in the Arts for the Disabled.* McLean, Va.: EPM Publications, 1988.

American Association for the Advancement of Science. *Barrier Free in Brief: Access to Science Literacy.* Washington, D.C.: American Association for the Advancement of Science, Project on Science, Technology, and Disability, 1991. (Also available in cassette form through Recording for the Blind.)

*Arts and Disabled People.* London: Bedford Square Press, for Carnegie United Kingdom Trust, 1985.

Association of Science-Technology Centers. *Access to Cultural Opportunities: Museums and the Handicapped.* Proceedings of the conference of the same name held on February 22–24, 1979 in Washington, D.C. Washington, D.C.: Association of Science-Technology Centers, 1980. 189 pp. bibliog.

Association of Science-Technology Centers. *Natural Partners: How Science Centers and Community Groups Can Team Up to Increase Science Literacy.* Proceedings of a workshop on the participation of women, minorities, and disabled people in science museums. Edited by Lynda Martin-McCormick. Washington, D.C.: Association of Science-Technology Centers and the American Association for Advance of Science, Office of Opportunities, 1987. 48 pp.

Berry, Nancy. "Special Audiences: Diagnosis and Treatment." In *Public View: The ICOM Handbook of Museum Public Relations*, pp. 26–33. Paris: ICOM, 1986.

Booth, Jeanette Hauck, Gerald Krockover, and Paula R. Woods. "Working with Special Groups." In *Creative Museum Methods and Educational Techniques*, pp. 104–18. Springfield: Charles C. Thomas, 1982.

Collins, Zipporah W., ed. *Museums, Adults and the Humanities: A Guide for Educational Programming*. Washington, D.C.: American Association of Museums, 1981. 399 pp.

Davidson, Betty. *Museum Exhibits and Programs: Are They Accessible to Disabled Users? A Model Evaluation Procedure*. Washington, D.C.: American Association for the Advancement of Science, Project on Science, Technology, and Disability, 1987.

Davidson, Betty. "The Special Needs Audience." In *New Dimensions for Traditional Dioramas: Multisensory Additions for Access, Interest and Learning*, pp. 50–58. Boston: Museum of Science, 1991. 82 pp.

Davidson, Betty. *People With Disabilities: An Untapped Source of Museum Volunteers*. Washington, D.C.: American Association for the Advancement of Science, Project on Science, Technology, and Disability, 1987.

Gosling, David. "Disabled Visitors." In *The Design of Educational Exhibits*, compiled by Roger S. Miles, in collaboration with M. B. Alt et al., pp. 102–05. 2d rev. edition. London and Boston: Allen & Unwin, 1988.

Hands-On Museums: *Partners in Learning*. Washington, D.C.: Educational Facilities Laboratories, for the National Endowment for the Arts, 1975.

Kamien, Janet. "How Do Special Needs Alter Arts Education Programs Outside the Regular Classroom Setting: An Example from the Children's Museum in Boston." In *The Arts Educator and Children with Special Needs: Conference Report*. Washington, D.C.: The National Committee, Arts for the Handicapped, 1978.

Kamien, Janet. *What If You Couldn't? A Book about Special Needs*. New York: Charles Scribner's Sons, 1979. 83 pp.

Kamien, Janet, and Amy Goldbas. *Museum Experiences for Families with Severely Disabled Kids. . . . A Program from The Boston Children's Museum*. Boston: The Boston Children's Museum, 1981. 31 pp.

Kennedy, Jeff. *User Friendly: Hands-On Exhibits That Work*. Washington, D.C.: Association of Science-Technology Centers, 1990.

Kenney, Alice P. "Compel Them to Come In." In *Museum Education Anthology 1973–1983*, pp. 78–82. Edited by Susan K. Nichols. Washington, D.C.: Museum Education Roundtable, 1984. 258 pp. (First published in *The Journal of Museum Education: Roundtable Reports* 6 (2): 3–4, 14 (1981).)

Majewski, Janice. *Part of Your General Public Is Disabled: A Handbook for Guides in Museums, Zoos, and Historic Houses*. Washington, D.C.: Smithsonian Institution Press, for Office of Elementary and Secondary Education, 1987. 83 pp. bibliog. (Also available is *Disabled Museum Visitors: Part of Your General Public*, a videotape in VHS, BETA, and 3/4″ formats and a manual in audio cassette and braille format.)

Matyas, Marsha Lakes, and Lynda Martin-McCormick. *1990 Survey for Participation in Science Centers by Underserved Groups.* Washington, D.C.: Association of Science-Technology Centers, forthcoming.

Mertz, Greg. *An Object in the Hand: Museum Educational Outreach for the Elderly, Incarcerated & Disabled.* Washington, D.C.: Smithsonian Institution Collaborative Educational Outreach Program, 1981. 64 pp.

The Metropolitan Museum of Art. *Help for the Special Educator: Taking a Field Trip to The Metropolitan Museum of Art.* New York: The Metropolitan Museum of Art, 1981. 40 pp.

The Metropolitan Museum of Art. *Museums and the Disabled.* New York: The Metropolitan Museum of Art, 1979. 44 pp., bibliog.

The Metropolitan Museum of Art. *Standards for Signs and Labels in The Metropolitan Museum of Art.* New York: The Metropolitan Museum of Art. In preparation.

Munley, Mary Ellen, and Jeff Hayward. *Museums: Opening Doors and Expanding Awareness.* Washington, D.C.: Smithsonian Institution, National Museum of American Art, 1989.

*Museums Without Barriers: A New Deal for the Disabled.* Papers presented at a conference organized by Fondation de France on November 7–8, 1988 in Paris. London and New York: Routledge, 1991. bibliog.

National Endowment for the Arts and The President's Committee on Employment of the Handicapped. *Profiles in the Arts.* Edited by Marcia Sartwell. Washington, D.C.: U.S. Government Printing Office, 1986. 70 pp.

Newsome, Barbara Y., Adele Z. Silver, eds. "Museums and Community: Special Audiences." In *The Art Museum as Educator: A Collection of Studies to Practice and Policy,* pp. 159–176. Berkeley, Calif.: University of California Press, 1978. 830 pp.

Ontario Ministry of Citizenship and Culture. "The Community Museum and the Disabled Visitor." *Ontario Museum Notes: Practical Information on Operating a Community Museum,* no. 12. Toronto, Ontario: Ontario Ministry of Citizenship and Culture, 1985.

Owen, Mary Jane, ed. *Developing Museum Experiences for the Handicapped: A Gathering of Information Related to the Question of Accommodation and Accessibility within Museums.* Oakland, Calif.: The Western Association of Museums, 1978.

Park, David C., Wendy M. Ross, and W. Kay Ellis. *Interpretation for Disabled Visitors in the National Park System.* Washington, D.C.: U.S. National Park Service, Special Programs and Populations Branch, 1986. 107 pp.

Pearson, Anne. *Arts for Everyone: Guidance on Provision for Disabled People.* London: Carnegie United Kingdom Trust and Centre on Environment for the Handicapped, 1985. 110 pp.

Scottish Museums Council. *Museums Are for People.* Edinburgh: HMSO, 1985.

The Smithsonian Institution. *Museums and Handicapped Students: Guidelines for Educators.* Washington, D.C.: Smithsonian Institution, 1977. 163 pp., bibliog.

Sorrell, D. S., ed. *Museums and the Handicapped.* Seminar organized by the Group for Educational Services in Museums, Departments of Museum Studies and Adult Education, University of Leicester, England. Leicester, England: Leicestershire Museums, Art Galleries, and Records Service, 1976. 68 pp., bibliog.

*This Way Please: For Easier Access to the Arts, Helping Clients with Disability.* Edinburgh: Artlink and Scottish Arts Council, 1989. 4 pp.

*The Use of Museums by Disabled People. CEH Seminar. Some Practical Considerations.* London: Centre for Environment for the Handicapped, and Royal National Institute for the Blind, 1980.

~~~~~~~~~

## Journals

Bardt-Pellerin, Elisabeth. "An Experiment: Guiding Handicapped Children in the Museum." *Gazette* 14 (1–2): 18–30 (1981).

Bark, Lois. "Museum Experience for the Exceptional Child." *Museum News* 46 (2): 33–35 (1967).

Burkhalter, Bettye B., and Alexia M. Kartis. "Planning the Recreational-Educational Complex of the Alabama Space and Rocket Center." *CEFP Journal* 21: 13–15 (January-February 1983).

Callow, Kathy B. "Museums and the Disabled." *Museums Journal* 74 (2): 70–72 (1974).

Cook, Allison D. "New York City's Community Art Resource for Disabled Persons." *New York Community Art Resource* 3 (387): (December 1984).

"Focus on the Disabled: Challenge for Museums: Identifying and Defining the Task, Issue I." Special issue edited by Susan N. Lehman with Janice Majewski. *Roundtable Reports: The Journal of Museum Education* 6 (2): (1981).

"Focus on the Disabled Museum Visitor: Solutions Offered, Programs Described, and Resources Listed." Special issue edited by Susan N. Lehman with Janice Majewski. *Roundtable Reports: The Journal of Museum Education* 6 (3): (1981).

Gee, Maureen. "The Power to Act." *Museum* 33 (3): 133–38 (1981).

Harrison, Molly. "Handicapped Children and Museums." *Museums Journal* 59 (5): 101–102 (1959).

Heath, Alison M. "Common Sense, Patience and Enthusiasm." *Museum* 33 (3): 139–45 (1981).

Heath, Alison M. "The Same Only More So: Museums and the Handicapped Visitor." *Museums Journal* 76 (2): 56–58 (1976).

Heakes, Norma. "Serving the Handicapped." *Toronto Royal Ontario Museum Journal* 1: (Spring 1966).

Inglis, Robin R. "Editorial: Museums and the Handicapped." *Gazette* 11 (3): 2–6 (1978).

Judson, Bay. "Special Needs Students at the Museum of Art." *Carnegie Magazine* 55 (9): 34–37 (1981).

Kamien, Janet. "A Question of Accessibility." In special issue "Focus on the Disabled" edited by Susan N. Lehman with Janice Majewski. *The Journal of Museum Education: Roundtable Reports* 6 (2): 5–7 (1981).

Keen, Carolyn. "Visitor Services and People with a Disability." *Museums Journal* 84 (1): 33–38 (1984).

Kelly, Elisabeth. "New Services for the Disabled in American Museums." *Museums Journal* 82 (3): 157–59 (1982).

Kenney, Alice P. "Museums Are for You." *Lifeprints:* 17–23 (April–March 1984).

Kenney, Alice P. et al. "The Challenge for Museums: Identifying and Defining the Task." *Roundtable Reports: The Journal of Museum Education* 6 (2): 3–7, 14 (1981).

Madden, Joan C., and Judith White. "Joining Forces: Reaching Out to Special Audiences." *Museum News* 60 (4): 38–41 (1982).

Marez Oyens, Johannes de. "Nine Varieties of Handicap." *Museum* 33 (3): 158–59 (1981).

Marti, Laurent. "For the Future: The International Red Cross Museum in Geneva." *Museum* 33 (3): 194–96 (1981).

Mims, Sandra K. "Art Museums and Special Audiences." *School Arts* 81 (7): 32–33 (1982).

Molloy, Larry. "Museum Accessibility: The Continuing Dialog." *Museum News* 60 (2): 50–57 (1981).

"Museums and Disabled Persons." Special issue. *Museum* 33 (3): 125–95 (1981).

"Museums and Disabled People." Special issue edited by Camilla Boodle. *Museum News: The Journal of National Heritage, The Museums Action Movement, London* 45: (Autumn 1989). 8 pp.

Palmer, Cheryl P. "Accessibility for All." *SEMC Journal:* 9–14 (1979).

Paskowsky, Michael. "Accommodating the Disabled: How Much Is Enough?" *The Interpreter* 18 (3): 16–19 (1987).

Pearson, Anne. "The Vicious Circle: Museum Education and Handicapped People in Some London Museums." *Journal of Education in Museums* 3: 5–7 (1982).

Plominska, Sophia M. "Glimpses of Special Activities in Poland." *Museum* 33 (3): 183–85 (1981).

Rheaume, Paul H. "A Hands-On Approach for Don't Touch Exhibits." *Curator* 31 (2): 96–98 (1988).

Sharpe, Elizabeth. "Docents Experience Museum Visit as Disabled Visitors." In special issue "Focus on the Disabled Museum Visitor" edited by Susan N. Lehman with Janice Majewski. *The Journal of Museum Education: Roundtable Reports* 6 (3): 6–7 (1981).

Snider, Harold. "The Inviting Air of an Accessible Space." *Museum News* 55 (3): 18–20 (1977).

Terry, Paula. "New Rules Will Require Even Greater Access to Museums." *Museum News* 69 (1): 26–28 (1990).

Tillett, Susan P. "Private Museum Makes Accessibility Commitment." In special issue "Focus on the Disabled Museum Visitor" edited by Susan N. Lehman with Janice Majewski. *The Journal of Museum Education: Roundtable Reports* 6 (3): 2, 8, 12–14 (1981).

Treff, Hans-Albert. "Educating the Public." Special issue on Museums and Disabled Persons. *Museum* 33 (3): 151–155 (1981).

Tsuruta, Soichiro. "Adaptations in Japan." Special issue on Museums and Disabled Persons. *Museum* 33 (3): 185–187 (1981).

VISUAL IMPAIRMENTS

*Books, reports, and guides*

American Foundation for the Blind. *Nature Trails, Braille Trails, Fragrance Gardens: Touch Museums for the Blind: Policy Statement.* New York: American Foundation for the Blind, 1973.

*Appreciation of Art and Cultural Heritage.* Glasgow: Royal National Institute for the Blind and EBU Commission on Cultural Affairs, 1991.

Arts Education for the Blind. *AEB Newsletter: New Methodology for Museum Accessibility.* Whitney Museum, New York.

*Arts for Blind and Visually Impaired People.* New York: Educational Facilities Laboratories, 1978.

Coles, Peter. *Please Touch: An Evaluation of the "Please Touch" Exhibition at the British Museum, 31st March to 8th May 1983.* Dunfermline, Fife: Committee of Inquiry into the Arts and Disabled People, 1984.

*Directory of Museums with Facilities for Visually Handicapped People.* London: Royal National Institute for the Blind, 1988. 31 pp.

Duncan, John, Calasha Gish, Mary Ellen Mulholland, and Alex Townsend. *Environmental Modifications for the Visually Impaired: A Handbook.* New York: American Foundation for the Blind, 1977.

Freeman, F. *Shape and Form: A Tactile Exploration.* New York: Metropolitan Museum of Art, 1977.

Groff, Gerda, with Laura Garner. *What Museum Guides Need to Know: Access for*

*Blind and Visually Impaired Visitors.* New York: American Foundation for the Blind, 1989. 55 pp., bibliog.

Hulser, Richard P. *Mainstreaming the Visually Handicapped in the Hall of Meteorites, Minerals and Gems at the American Museum of Natural History,* 1979.

Kelley, Jerry D. *Recreation Programming for Visually Impaired Children and Youth.* New York: American Foundation for the Blind, 1981.

Lisenco, Yasha. *Art Not by Eye: The Previously Sighted Visually Impaired Adult in Fine Arts Programs.* New York: American Foundation for the Blind, 1971.

*The Museum and the Visually Impaired: The Report of the Work Group on Facilities for the Visually Impaired.* Toronto, Canada: Royal Ontario Museum, 1980.

Pearson, Anne, and Marcus Weisen. *Talking Touch. Proceedings of a conference at the Royal National Institute for the Blind on the Use of Touch in Museums and Galleries.* London: Royal National Institute for the Blind, 1988.

*Perceiving Modern Sculpture: Selections for the Sighted and Nonsighted.* New York: New York University, Grey Art Gallery and Study Center. 1980.

Rodriguez, S. "An Art Program for Visually Impaired Children." In *Prism: The Arts and the Handicapped.* Pittsburgh, Pa.: Museum of Art, Carnegie Institute, 1981.

Royal Ontario Museum. *The Museum and the Visually Impaired: The Report of the Work Group on Facilities for the Visually Impaired.* Toronto, Ontario: Royal Ontario Museum, 1980. 23 pp. bibliog.

Shore, Irma, and Beatrice Jacinto. *Access to Art: A Museum Directory for Blind and Visually Impaired People.* New York: American Foundation for the Blind and Museum of American Folk Art, 1989. 129 pp., bibliog.

Sheets, Ruth A. "Becoming Involved in the Museum Experience." In *New Attitudes at the Museum,* edited by Dana Walker, pp. 9–11. Washington, D.C.: American Council for the Blind, 1985. 26 pp.

Stanford, Charles W. *Art for Humanity's Sake: The Story of the Mary Duke Biddle Gallery for the Blind.* Raleigh, N.C.: North Carolina Museum of Art, 1976.

Stukey, Kenneth. "Experiencing the Museum." In *New Attitudes at the Museum,* edited by Dana Walker, pp. 12–15. Washington, D.C.: American Council of the Blind, 1985. 26 pp.

*Talking Touch: Report on a Seminar on the Use of Touch in Museums and Galleries Held at the Royal National Institute for the Blind on 29th February 1988.* Jointly organized with Museums and Galleries Disability Association (MAGDA). London: Royal National Institute for the Blind, 1988. 50 pp.

Walker, Dana, ed. *New Attitudes at the Museum.* Panel Discussion held in Philadelphia, Pennsylvania on July 2, 1984. Philadelphia: American Council of the Blind, Friends in Art, 1985.

Weisen, Marcus, and David Hammond. *Proposal for a Tactile Museum of Environmental Discovery*. London: Royal National Institute for the Blind, 1987. 95 pp., 7 appendices, bibliog.

Wexell, Astrid. "Tactile Pictures in Stockholm." *Museum* 33 (3): 180–83 (1981).

~~~~~~~~

## Journals

Alphen, Jan van. "Along the Tigris and the Euphrates." The Art Horizons, 1990: Report of European Blind Union Conference in *International Journal of Museum Management and Curatorship* 4 (3): 295–6 (1985).

"An Art Gallery for the Blind." *Programs for the Handicapped* 75 (8): 11–13 (1975).

Astone, Judy, Carolyn O. Blackmon, Joseph Buckley, and William Ingersol. "Setting Priorities." *Museum News* 55 (3): 30–31, 45 (1977).

Bartlett, J. E. "Museums and the Blind." *Museums Journal* 54 (11): (1959).

Bateman, Penny. "Human Touch" British Museum Exhibition 6 Feb. to 16 March 1986, Comments and Ideas." *British Journal of Visual Impairment* 4: 77–79 (Summer 1986).

Bourgeois-Lechartier, Michel. "At Lons-le-Saunier (France). Friendship: The Most Powerful Force." *Museum* 33 (3): 160–65 (1981).

Bronsdon Rowan, Madeline, and Sally Rogow. "Making Museums Meaningful for Blind Children." *Gazette* 11 (3): 36–41 (1978).

Byrne, S. "Design for a Mobile, Audio-Tactile Exhibition for Blind and Sighted School-Age Children." *The New Outlook for the Blind* 68 (6): 252–59 (1974).

Calhoun, Sally N. "On the Edge of Vision." *Museum News* 52 (7): 36–41 (1974).

Covington, George A. "Photography Aids Visually Impaired Museum Visitors." In special issue "Focus on the Disabled" edited by Susan N. Lehman with Jan Majewski. *Roundtable Reports: The Journal of Museum Education* 6 (2): 6–7 (1981).

Cronk, Michael Sam. "Blindness and the Museum Experience." *Ontario Museum Quarterly, Toronto* (12) 3: 13–15 (September 1983).

Delevoy-Otlet, S. "A Museum for the Blind: The Royal Museums of Art and History, Brussels." *Museum* 28 (3): 178–80 (1976).

De Wyngaert, Laura. "Art for the Blind. . . . " *Arts and Activities* 73: 30–32 (1973).

Duczmal-Pacowska, Halina. "The Museum and the Blind." *Museum* 28 (3):176 (1976).

Duczmal-Pacowska, Halina. "Why Not Science Exhibitions for the Blind? *Museum* 28 (3): 176–77 (1976).

Duncan, John et al. "Environmental Modifications for the Visually Impaired." *Journal of Visual Impairment & Blindness* 71 (10): 442–55 (1977).

Favière, Jean. "The Museum and the Blind: Introduction." *Museum* 28 (3): 176 (1976).

Favière, Jean, Halina Duczmal, and S. Delevoy-Otlet. "The Museum and the Blind." *Museum* 28 (3): 172–76 (1976).

Ford Smith, James. "A Sense of Touch." *Museums Journal*, 83 (2–3): 143 (1983).

Freer, Margaret E. "An Art Experience through Touch." *Braille Forum* 11 (5): 3–6 (1973).

Goldberg, Joshua. "In Praise of Darkness: The 'Hands-on Japan' Exhibition." *Museum* 33 (3): 187–92 (1981).

Haseltine, James L. "Please Touch." *Museum News* 45 (2): 11–16 (1966).

Henriksen, Harry C. "Your Museum: A Resource for the Blind." *Museum News* 50 (2): 26–28 (1971).

Hunt, Susan. "An Exhibit for Touching." *Journal of Visual Impairment & Blindness* 73 (9): 364–66 (1979).

Kenney, Alice P. "A Range of Vision: Museum Accommodations for Visually Impaired People." *Journal of Visual Impairment & Blindness* 77 (7): 325–29 (1983).

Kolar, Judith Rena. "A Bird in the Hand: Planning a Zoo Program for the Blind." *Curator* 24 (2): 97–108 (1981).

Lehon, Lester H. "Development of Lighting Standards for the Visually Impaired." *Journal of Visual Impairment & Blindness* 74 (7): 249–53 (1980).

Libin, Laurence. "To Touch and Hear: A Musical Instruments Exhibition for the Blind." *ICOM Education*, ICOM-CECA 7: 36–37 (1975–76).

Maynard, Merrill A. "Museums Are a Resource for the Blind." *Dialogue* 24 (3): 83–84 (1985).

Moore, George. "Displays for the Sightless." *Curator* 11 (4): 292–96 (1968).

Nair, S. N. "Special Programmes for Blind Children at the National Museum of Natural History, New Delhi, India." *Museum* 33 (3): 174–75 (1981).

Pearson, Anne. "Please Touch: An Exhibition of Animal Sculpture at the British Museum." *International Journal of Museum Management and Curatorship* 3 (4): 373–78 (1984).

Pearson, Fiona. "Sculpture for the Blind: National Museum of Wales." *Museums Journal* 81 (1): 35–37 (1981).

Pierotti, R. "Be, See, Touch, Respond." *Museum News* 52: 43–48 (1973).

Raffay, Monique. "The Arts through Touch Perception: Present Trends and Future Prospects." *British Journal of Visual Impairment* 6 (2): 63–65 (1988).

Rowan, Madeline B., and Sally Rogow. "Making Museums Meaningful for Blind Children." *Gazette* 11 (3): 36–41 (1978).

Rowland, William. "An Experiment in Art Appreciation by Touch." *New Beacon* 58 (685): 115–17 (1974).

Rowland, William. "Museums and the Blind: It Feels Like a Flower . . ." *ICOM News* 26 (3): 117–21 (1973).

Rubin, Judith A. "The Exploration of a 'Tactile Aesthetic'." *New Outlook for the Blind* 70 (9): 369–75 (1976).

Scherf-Smith, Patricia. "Against Segregating the Blind." *Museum News* 55 (3): 10–11 (1977).

Seven, Steven M. "Environmental Interpretation for the Visually Impaired." *Education of the Visually Handicapped* 12: 53–58 (Summer 1980).

Sheets, R. A. "Sharing the Museum Experience." *Braille Forum* 23: 12–16 (January 1985).

Shore, Irma. "Designing Exhibits for the Visually Impaired." *Museum News* 67 (2): 62–64 (1988).

Snider, Harold. "Arts for the Blind and Visually Impaired: A View from the Jungle." *The Braille Monitor:* 40–43 (February 1978).

Snider, Harold. "Museum Integration." *The New Beacon* 61 (719). London: Royal Institute for the Blind.

Snider, Harold. "Museums and the Blind: A Look Ahead." *The Braille Monitor:* 465–67 (September 1976).

Stanford, Charles W. "Knowing Art in a Museum through the Perception of Touch." *North Carolina Art Museum Bulletin* 8 (2): 4–11 (1968).

Stanford, Charles W. "A Museum Gallery for the Blind." *Museum News* 44 (10): 18–23 (1966).

Steiner, Charles K. "Art Museums and the Visually Handicapped Consumer: Some Issues in Approach and Design." *Journal of Visual Impairment & Blindness* 77 (7): 330–33 (1983).

Steiner, Charles K., Amy German, Wolfgang Brolley, "Helping Hearing-Disabled Visitors and the Metropolitan Museum of Art." *Their World*, 1982. (Publication of Foundation for Children with Hearing Disabilities)

"The Tactual Museum of Athens: An Educational Resource for the Blind." *Museum*(162): 78–79 (1989).

Toll, Dove. "Should Museums Serve the Visually Handicapped?" *The New Outlook for the Blind* 69 (10): 461–64 (1975).

Watkins, Malcolm J. "A Small Handling Table for Blind Visitors." *Museums Journal* 75 (1): 29–30 (1975).

HEARING IMPAIRMENTS

*Books, reports, and guides*

Banks, Geraldine, and Mary Pulsifer. "Good Impressions." *Perspectives for Teachers of the Hearing Impaired* 4 (3): 6–9 (1986).

Bergman, Eugene. *Arts Accessibility for the Deaf.* Washington, D.C.: National Access Center, 1981. 24 pp.

Bizaguet, Eric. "Sufferers from Defective Hearing and the New Techniques for Communication." In *Museums without Barriers: A New Deal for the Disabled*, pp. 156–59. London and New York: Routledge, 1991.

Bouchauveau, Guy. "Reception Services for the Deaf at the Cité des Sciences et de l'Industrie at La Villette in Paris." In *Museums without Barriers: A New Deal for the Disabled*, pp. 160–62. London and New York: Routledge, 1991.

Derycke, Beatrice. "International Visual Art for the Deaf." In *Museums without Barriers: A New Deal for the Disabled*, pp. 163–164. London and New York: Routledge, 1991.

Fellman, Meri. *Programs for Deaf Visitors at the National Air and Space Museum: Research Study.* Washington, D.C.: Smithsonian Institution, National Air and Space Museum, 1977.

Harkness, Sarah P. *Building Without Barriers for the Disabled.* New York: Whitney Library of Design, 1976.

Landmark Society of Western New York. *Museums Are for Everyone: Accessibility for the Hearing Impaired.* Rochester, N.Y.: The Landmark Society of Western New York, 1982.

Morgan, Michelle. *Notes on Design Criteria for People with Deafness.* Washington, D.C.: The American Institute of Architects, 1976.

*Sign-Language Program.* New York: The Metropolitan Museum of Art, Division of Education Services, Spring 1989.

Walker, Lou Ann, and Nancy Rosenblatt Richner. *Museum Accessibility for Hearing-Impaired People.* New York: The Modern Museum of Art, 1983. 97 pp.

Willard, Tom. *Arts and Museum Accessibility for Deaf and Hard of Hearing People.* Rochester, N.Y.: Deaf Artists of America, 1991. 32 pp.

~~~~~~~~~~

## Journals

Breunig, H. Latham. "About the Hearing-Impaired Audience." In special issue "Focus on the Disabled" edited by Susan N. Lehman with Janice Majewski. *The Journal of Museum Education: Roundtable Reports* 6 (2): 9–11 (1981).

Feeley, Jennifer. "The 'Listening Eye': Tours for the Deaf in San Francisco Bay Area Museums." *Museum Studies Journal* 2 (1): 36–49 (1985).

Novik, Sandra P. "Museum Characteristics Advantageous for Education of the Deaf." *Journal for the Rehabilitation of the Deaf* 17 (3): 5–12 (1983).

Sutherland, Mimi. "Total Communication." *Museum News* 55 (3): 24–26 (1977).

Tennenbaum, Paula. "Soundtracks: Intern Develops New Audiences." *The Museologist* 46 (167): 8–10 (Spring 1984).

*Books, reports, and guides*

Artymowski, Jan D. "Services for the Mentally Handicapped at the Royal Castle in Warsaw, Poland." In *Museums without Barriers: A New Deal for the Disabled*, pp. 181–186. London and New York: Routledge, 1991.

de Ponthieu, Jean. "Art and Museums Even for Those Who Suffer the Worst Disadvantage." In *Museums without Barriers: A New Deal for the Disabled*, pp. 167–171. London and New York: Routledge, 1991.

The Metropolitan Museum of Art. *Museum Education for Retarded Adults: Reaching Out to a Neglected Audience*. New York: The Metropolitan Museum of Art, 1979. 47 pp. bibliog.

Reising, Gert. "The National Museum of Fine Arts in Karlsruhe, Germany." In *Museums without Barriers: A New Deal for the Disabled*, pp. 177–180. London and New York: Routledge, 1991.

Steiner, Charles K. "Museum Programmes Designed for Mentally Disabled Visitors." In *Museums without Barriers: A New Deal for the Disabled*, pp. 172–176. London and New York: Routledge, 1991.

Steiner, Charles K. *Museums: A Resource for the Learning Disabled*. 2d ed. New York: The Metropolitan Museum of Art, Division of Education Services, 1984. 32 pp.

Steiner, Charles K., Amy German, and Wolfgang Brolley. "Helping Learning Disabled Visitors at the Metropolitan Museum of Art." In *Their World*, pp. 76–77. New York: Foundation for Children with Learning Disabilities, 1983.

*Journals*

Ouertani, Nayla. "A New Source of Hope: A Scheme for Mentally Handicapped Children in Tunisia." *Museum* 33 (3): 172–173 (1981).

Schleien, Stuart J. et al. "Integrating Children with Moderate to Severe Cognitive Deficits into a Community Museum Program." *Education and Training in Mental Retardation* 22 (2): 112–20 (1987).

Steiner, Charles K. "Reaching the Mentally Handicapped." *Museum News* 56 (6): 19–23 (1978).

Steiner, Charles K. "The Met and Mentally Retarded Museum-Goers." In special issue "Focus on the Disabled" edited by Susan N. Lehman with Janice Majewski. *The Journal of Museum Education* 6 (3): 7–8 (1981).

*Books, reports, and guides*

Richard, Anne. *Able to Attend: A Good Practice Guide on Access to Events for Disabled People.* London: NCVO Employment Unit, 1987. 30 pp.

The Smithsonian Institution. *Smithsonian: A Guide for Disabled Visitors.* Washington, D.C.: Smithsonian Institution, 1989. 27 pp.

*Journals*

Ashby, Helen. "York 'Please Touch' Workshop." *Museums Journal* 89 (8): 11 (1989).

Kenney, Alice P. "Museums from a Wheelchair." *Museum News* 53 (4): 14–17 (1974).

Kenney, Alice P. "A Test of Barrier-Free Design." *Museum News* 55 (3): 27–29 (1977).

Westerlund, Stella, and Thomas Knuthammar. "Handicaps Prohibited—Travelling Exhibition in Sweden." Museum 33 (3): 176–79 (19082).

*Books, reports, and guides*

American Association of Retired Persons. *Attracting Older Americans to Museums: A Guide for Museum Educators.* Washington, D.C.: American Association of Retired Persons, Institute of Lifetime Learning, 1985. 28 pp.

American Association of Retired Persons. *Museum Opportunities for Older Persons.* Washington, D.C.: American Association of Retired Persons, 1984. 16 pp.

*Art, the Elderly, and a Museum: Older Adult Programs at the Brooklyn Museum.* Brooklyn, N.Y.: The Brooklyn Museum, 1980.

Balkema, John B., with Harry R. Moody. *The Creative Spirit: An Annotated Bibliography on the Arts, Humanities and Aging.* Washington, D.C.: The National Council on Aging, 1986.

Cahill, Pati, comp. *Arts, the Humanities and Older Americans: A Catalogue of Program Profiles.* Washington, D.C.: The National Council on the Aging, 1981, 81 pp.

Greenberg, Pearl, with Paula Terry. *Visual Arts and Older People: Developing Quality Programs.* Springfield, Ill.: Charles C. Thomas, 1987. 205 pp.

Heffernan, Ildiko, and Sandra Schnee. *Art, the Elderly, and a Museum: Older Adult Programs at the Brooklyn Museum.* Brooklyn, N.Y.: The Brooklyn Museum, 1980.

Johnson, Alton C., and E. Arthur Prieve. *Older Americans: The Unrealized Audience for the Arts.* Madison: University of Wisconsin, 1977.

McCutcheon, Priscilla B. *An Arts and Aging Media Sourcebook: Films, Videos, Slide/Tape Shows.* Washington, D.C.: The National Council on the Aging, 1986.

McCutcheon, Priscilla B., and Cathryn S. Wolf. *A Resource Guide to People, Places and Programs in Arts and Aging.* Washington, D.C.: The National Council on the Aging, 1984. 188 pp.

Mertz, Gregory A., with illustrations by Sara Stromayer. *Our Natural World: Group Discussion and Activity Guides for Older Audiences and Their Group Leaders.* Washington, D.C.: Office of Education, National Museum of American History, Smithsonian Institution, 1986. 96 pp.

*Older Adults in Museums, Arts and Humanities: Selected Readings and Resources.* Washington, D.C.: Smithsonian Institution, Museum Reference Center, 1984.

Padwe, Alice, ed. *Older Adults and the Museum World: An Emerging Partnership.* Washington, D.C.: Smithsonian Institution, 1982. 66 pp., bibliog.

Rubin, Eleanor. *Looking Together: A Free Training Program for Senior Adults at the Museum of Fine Arts, Boston.* Boston: Museum of Fine Arts, 1979. 103 pp.

*Senior Citizen Program—The Baltimore Museum of Art: A Handbook.* Baltimore, Md.: The Baltimore Museum of Art, Division of Education, Senior Citizen Program, 1977.

Sharpe, Elizabeth M. *The Senior Series Program: A Case Study with Implications for Adoption.* Washington, D.C.: Smithsonian Institution, National Museum of American History, 1982. 228 pp.

## Journals

Graetz, Linda. "Houston: 'A Steady Hand and Peaceful Heart'" in a special section "Art Museums and Older Adults." *Museum News* 59 (5): 30, 33–35 (1981).

Heffernan, Ildiko, and Sandra Schnee. "Brooklyn: Building a New Musuem Audience" in special section "Art Museums and Older Adults." *Museum News* 59 (5): 30–32 (1981).

Hubbard, Linda. "Partners in Learning." *Modern Maturity* 26 (1): 87–88 (1983).

"Museums and Older Adults." Special issue edited by Elizabeth M. Sharpe et al. *Roundtable Reports: The Journal of Museum Education* 9 (4): 2–20 (Fall 1984).

Sunderland, Jacqueline T. "Museums and Older Americans." *Museum News* 55 (3): 21–23 (1977).

*Books, reports, and guides*

*Access Improvements in Historic Districts: Providing Access to Boston's Historic New-
bury Street for People with Disabilities.* Boston, Mass.: Design Guild Adaptive Environments Center, 1989.

Ballantyne, Duncan S. *Accommodation of Disabled Visitors at Historic Sites in the
National Park System.* Washington, D.C.: U.S. Department of the Interior, Technical Preservation Services Division, 1983.

*Cultural Resources Management Guideline*, no. NPS-28. Washington, D.C.: U.S. Department of the Interior, National Park System, Park Historic Architecture Division, Cultural Resources Management, 1985.

Battaglia, David H. *The Impact of the Americans with Disabilities Act on Historic
Structures. Information Series*, no. 55. Washington, D.C.: National Trust for
Historic Preservation, 1991. 16 pp.

Battaglia, David H. "Americans with Disabilities Act: Its Impact on Historic Buildings and Structures." 10 *Preservation Law Reporter* 1169 (1991).

Douglas, James D. "Requirements for Accessibility in Historic Buildings under
the Americans with Disabilities Act." In *Legal Problems of Museum Administration: Course of Study Transcripts*, cosponsored by The Smithsonian Institution with the Cooperation of the American Association of Museums, pp.
387–98. Washington, D.C.: The American Law Institute, 1992.

*The Impact of Accessibility and Historic Preservation Laws, Regulations and Poli-
cies on NPS Historic Sites: Analysis and Recommendations.* Washington, D.C.:
U.S. Department of the Interior, National Park Service, 1978.

Jester, Thomas C., and Judy L. Hayward, eds. *Accessibility and Historic Preservation Resource Guide.* A guide to The Accessibility and Historic Preservation
Workshops sponsored by the Historic Windsor; the National Park Service,
Preservation Assistance Division; the Advisory Council on Historic Preservation; and the National Conference of State Historic Preservation Officers. Photocopy, 1992. Reprint information available from Historic Windsor, Inc., Windsor, Vt.

Kenney, Alice P. *Hospitable Heritage: The Report of Museum Access.* Allentown,
Pa.: Lehigh County Historical Society, 1979. 44 pp.

Kenney, Alice P., with Charles Cox. *Access to the Past: Museum Programs and
Handicapped Visitors. A Guide to Section 504—Making Existing Programs and
Facilities Accessible to the Disabled Person.* Nashville, Tenn.: American Asso-
ciation for State and Local History, 1980. 131 pp., bibliog.

Parrott, Charles. *Access to Historic Buildings for the Disabled: Suggestions for Planning and Implementation*, no. 46. Washington, D.C.: U.S. Department of the Interior, Technical Preservation Services Division, 1980. 86 pp.

Smith, William, and Tara G. Frier. *Access to History: A Guide to Providing Access to Historic Buildings for People with Disabilities.* Boston, Mass.: Massachusetts Historical Commission, 1989.

"Preserving the Past and Making It Accessible to Everyone: How Easy a Task?" *CRM Supplement 1991.* Washington, D.C.: U.S. Department of the Interior, National Park Service, Preservation Assistance Division, Cultural Resources Programs, 1991.

U.S. Department of the Interior, National Park Service. *Accommodation of Handicapped Visitors at Historic Sites*, Volume 1 Guide and Volume 2 Technical Manual. Washington, D.C.: Government Printing Office, 1979.

~~~~~~~

### Journals

"Access to History." *Historic Preservation* 30 (3): 2–3 (1978).

Artymowsky, Daniel. "A Calling and a Challenge: Working for the Handicapped at the Royal Castle in Warsaw." *The International Journal of Museum Management and Curatorship* 5 (2): 159–62 (1986).

Kenney, Alice P. "Open Door for the Handicapped." *Historic Preservation* 30 (3): 12–17 (1978).

James, Marianna S. "One Step at a Time: How Winterthur Approaches Program Accessibility." *History News* 36 (7): 10–15 (1981). bibliog.

Walter, J. Jackson. "President's Note." An editorial on making the seventeen properties of the National Trust for Historic Preservation accessible to the disabled. *Historic Preservation* 42 (3): 6 (1990).

### PLANNING, DESIGNING, FUNDING, AND BUILDING ACCESSIBLE MUSEUMS

~~~~~~~~~~~~~~~~~~~~~~~~~~~~~~

### Books, reports, and guides

"The Adapt Fund: Guidelines." In *Adapt: Access for Disabled People to Arts Premises Today.* Dunfermline, England: Carnegie United Kingdom Trust, 1990.

*Community Development Block Grant Report.* Photocopy. (Available from the National Endowment for the Arts, 1989, 1992 [forthcoming]).

Danilov, Victor J. *Science and Technology Centers.* Cambridge: The MIT Press, 1982. 363 pp.

*Getting There: A Guide to Accessibility for Your Facility.* Berkeley, Calif.: Center for Planning and Development Research, State of California Department of Vocational Rehabilitation, 1979.

*Funding Sources and Technical Assistance for Museums and Historical Agencies.* Compiled by Hedy A. Hartman. Nashville, Tenn.: The American Association for State and Local History, 1979.

*Handicapped Funding Directory: A Guide to Sources of Funding in the United States for Handicapped Programs and Services for the Disabled.* Seventh edition. Margate, Fla.: Research Grant Guides, 1990.

*Management Policies.* Washington, D.C.: U.S. Department of the Interior, National Park Service, 1988.

Scott, Bruce H. *Book of Renovations: A Compilation of Drawings Depicting the Most Common Problems and Solutions to Renovating Existing Buildings and Facilities to Make Them Accessible to and Usable by People with Physical Disabilities.* Lawrence, Kans.: Kansas University, Research and Training Center on Independent Living, 1985.

Trippett, Laurie. "The Accessibility Standards and Where to Find Them." In *The Sourcebook 1992,* pp. 55–82. Washington, D.C.: The American Association of Museums, 1992.

## ARCHITECTURAL SPECIFICATIONS

### Books, reports, and guides

*The American Institute of Architects. Design for Aging: An Architect's Guide.* Washington, D.C.: The AIA Press, 1986, 1987.

American National Standards Institute. *American National Standards Specifications for Making Buildings and Facilities Accessible to and Usable by Physically Handicapped People,* no. A117.1 (rev. of ANSI A117.1–1961). New York: American National Standards Institute, 1980. 68 pp.

*The Americans with Disabilities Act: Accessibility Guidelines for Buildings and Facilities,* 36 CFR Part 1191, Sept. 6, 1991. Washington, D.C.: U.S. Architectural and Transportaiton Barriers Compliance Board. 28 pp.

Goldsmith, S. *Designing for the Disabled.* 3d ed. London: RIBA Publications, 1976.

Kliment, Stephen A. *Into the Mainstream: A Syllabus for a Barrier Free Environment.* Washington, D.C.: The American Institute of Architects, 1975.

Mace, Ronald L. *Accessibility Modifications: Guidelines for Modification of Existing Buildings for Accessibility to the Handicapped.* Raleigh, N.C.: Barrier-

Free Environments, for North Carolina Department of Insurance, Special Office for the Handicapped, 1976, 1979.

Mace, Ronald L. *Application of Basic Design Specifications.* Washington, D.C.: The American Institute of Architects, 1978.

Mace, Ronald L. et al. *The Planners Guide to Barrier-Free Meetings.* Waltham, Mass.: Barrier-Free Environments and Howard Russell Associates, 1980.

Milner, Margaret. *Opening Doors, A Handbook on Making Facilities Accessible to Handicapped People.* Washington, D.C.: National Center for a Barrier Free Environment and Community Services Administration, 1978.

*Uniform Federal Accessibility Standards*, 49 FR 31528 August 7, 1984. Washington, D.C.: U.S. Architectural and Transportation Barriers Compliance Board. 69 pp.

~~~~~~~~

## Journals

Jones, Michael A., and John H. Catlin. "Design for Access." *Progressive Architecture:* 65–70 (April 1978).

Townsend, Sally. "Touch and See—Architecture for the Blind." *Curator* 18 (3): 200–05 (1975)

Vorreiter, Gabrielle. "Theatre of Touch." *The Architectural Review*, London (1108): (1989).

### LEGAL REGULATIONS

~~~~~~~~~~~~~~~~~~~~~~~~~~~~~~~~

### Books, reports, and guides

*The ADA Handbook.* Washington, D.C.: EEOC and the U.S. Dept. of Justice, 1991.

*Americans with Disabilities Act: ADA Compliance Guide.* Washington, D.C.: Thompson Publishing Group, 1990.

*The Americans with Disabilities Act: From Policy to Practice.* Edited by Jane West. New York: Milbank Memorial Fund, 1991. 360 pp.

*American with Disabilities Act of 1990: Law and Explanation.* Chicago, Ill.: Commerce Clearing House, 1990.

*Americans with Disabilities Act Manual.* Washington, D.C.: The Bureau of National Affairs, 1992.

Catlin, John H, Loebl Schlossman, and Hackl, Inc. "Americans with Disabilities Act: Museum Compliance." In *Legal Problems of Museum Administration: Course of Study Transcripts*, cosponsored by The Smithsonian Institution with the Cooperation of the American Association of Museums, pp. 381–86. Washington, D.C.: The American Law Institute, 1992.

Cooke, Edmund D., and Peter S. Gray, eds. *The Disability Law Reporter Service.*

Englewood Cliffs, N.J.: Prentice Hall Law and Business, 1991.

General Services Administration, Department of Defense, Department of Housing and Urban Development, and U.S. Postal Service. *Uniform Federal Accessibility Standards.* Washington, D.C.: U.S. Government Printing Office, 1988.

Kamien, Janet, Amy Goldbas, and Susan Porter. *Is There Life After 504? A Guide to Building and Program Accessibility.* Boston: The Children's Museum, 1980, 1982. 42 pp.

National Center for Law and Deafness. "The Americans with Disabilities Act" and "Architectural Barriers" in *Legal Rights: The Guide for Deaf and Hard of Hearing People*, pp. 15–46 and pp. 167–72. 4th ed. Washington, D.C.: Gallaudet University Press, 1992. 297 pp.

National Endowment for the Arts. *The Arts and 504: A 504 Handbook for Accessible Arts Programming.* Raleigh, N.C.: Barrier-Free Environments, for the National Endowment for the Arts, 1985. 97 pp. (A twenty-two page companion publication is the *Program Evaluation Workbook*, available from the National Endowment for the Arts, Office for Special Constituencies.)

Naeve, Robert A. *Managing ADA: The Complete Compliance Guide.* New York: Wiley Law Publications, 1992.

*Regulations for Nondiscrimination on the Basis of Handicap under Section 504 of the Rehabilitation Act of 1973.* 44 Fed. Reg. 22730, April 17, 1979 and 45 C.F.R., part 1151. (Also available in large type for the visually impaired from the National Endowment of the Arts.)

*Summary of Existing Legislation Affecting Persons with Disabilities.* Washington, D.C.: U.S. Department of Education, Office of Special Education and Rehabilitative Services, Clearinghouse on the Handicapped, 1992.

*UFAS Retrofit Manual.* Washington, D.C.: U.S. Architectural and Transportation Barriers Compliance Board, 1991.

## Journals

Kamien, Janet. "A Question of Accessibility." In special issue "Focus on the Disabled" edited by Susan N. Lehman with Janice Majewski. *The Journal of Museum Education: Roundtable Reports* 6 (2): 5, 7 (1981).

Molloy, Larry. "504 Regs: Learning to Live by the Rules." *Museum News* 57 (1): 28–33 (1978).

Molloy, Larry. "The Case for Accessibility." *Museum News* 55 (3): 15–17 (1977).

Molloy, Larry. "One Way to Comply with Section 504." *Museum News* 57 (4): 24–28 (1979).

Olsen, Marion. "Programming and 504." *Museum News* 59 (4): 9, 11, 13–14, 16 (1981).

# Index